Canoeing and Kayaking Houston Waterways

CANOEING AND KAYAKING HOUSTON WATERWAYS

Natalie H. Wiest

Maps by Jerry Moulden
Foreword by Andrew Sansom

TEXAS A&M UNIVERSITY PRESS • *College Station*

Publication of this book was generously aided by a gift from the Jacob and Terese Hershey Foundation. The maps were created thanks to the generosity of Frank C. Smith, Jr. and Avon S. Duson of the Bayou Fund and a grant from the Bayou Preservation Association.

River Books
Sponsored by
 the River Systems Institute
at Texas State University
Andrew Sansom,
General Editor

A list of books in this series is available at the end of the book.

Copyright © 2012 by Natalie Wiest
Maps copyright © Shoreline Publishing
Manufactured in China by Everbest Printing Co.,
through FCI Print Group

First edition

This paper meets the requirements of
ANSI/NISO Z39.48-1992 (Permanence of Paper).
Binding materials have been chosen for durability.

LIBRARY OF CONGRESS
CATALOGING-IN-PUBLICATION DATA

Wiest, Natalie H., 1948–
Canoeing and kayaking Houston waterways /
Natalie H. Wiest ; maps by Jerry Moulden. — 1st ed.
    p. cm. — (River books) Includes bibliographical
references and index.
    ISBN-13: 978-1-60344-764-5 (flex : alk. paper)
    ISBN-10: 1-60344-764-4 (flex : alk. paper)
    ISBN-13: 978-1-60344-775-1 (e-book)
    ISBN-10: 1-60344-775-X (e-book)
    1. Canoes and canoeing—Texas, East—Guidebooks.
2. Rivers—Texas, East—Guidebooks. 3. Waterways—
Texas, East—Guidebooks. 4. Houston (Tex.)—Guidebooks.
5. Texas, East—Guidebooks. I. Title.
    GV776.T42W54   2012
    797.12209764—dc23
    2012017274

Chapter opening art created by Gary Gore

to Terry Hershey, who saved Houston's natural waterways

Contents

Terry Hershey at Four Mile Ranch. Photo by Brian Swett.

Foreword

AS SURELY AS HOUSTON is defined by the oil and gas industry; as surely as Texas' largest city is identified with humanity's first steps on the moon; Houston is identified and defined by its waterways and its bayous. The city began at the confluence of Buffalo and White Oak Bayous where, in 1836, the Allen Brothers first stepped ashore and founded Houston's first port. Today, as Natalie Wiest skillfully lays out in this eleventh volume of River Books, Allen's Landing is part of a remarkable system of natural and cultural amenities associated with the city's watercourses that provide a rich and exciting venue for outdoor recreation and exploration.

Through the years, no name has been more identified with the defining feature of the Bayou City than that of Terry Hershey. Herself a true force of nature, Mrs. Hershey became alarmed that the cement channelization that had destroyed the natural beauty of Brays and White Oak bayous would also consume her beloved Buffalo Bayou. Vowing to ensure that the meandering integrity of the bayou would not be destroyed, she enlisted the help of oilman George Mitchell and a young Republican congressman named George H. W. Bush. With the help of the men she calls the "Two Georges," Terry was successful in deleting funding for the "improvement" of Buffalo Bayou from the federal budget and thus saved the bayou from ruin.

When I returned to Texas in the late 1970s from Washington, DC, I was told that Terry Hershey was one of the most important environmental leaders in Texas and a person I must meet. For the last forty years, she has been one of my heroes. Terry not only changed the entire culture of Houston with respect to the care and management of its bayous, she founded most of the city's conservation organizations, including the Citizens' Environmental Coalition, the Bayou Preservation Association, and the Park People (now part of the Houston Parks Board).

Terry and her late husband, Jake, created the Jacob and Terese Hershey Foundation, one of Texas' leading environmental philanthropies. Inspired by her love of nature and its "critters," the Hershey Foundation has helped make possible some of the state's most significant conservation initiatives, including the Texas Land Trust Council and many more worthy efforts, including this book.

Thanks to Terry's support, here on these pages, the bayous and waterways of Houston are described in detail for the benefit of all who would seek a deeper level of appreciation for them and the pleasures and challenges they have to offer. I hope you will find Natalie Wiest's work a springboard to your enjoyment of them. As you wind through their twists and turns, I hope you will take the opportunity to reflect that had it not been for one extraordinary woman, these beautiful natural settings would all be lined with cement.

So enjoy the bayous and waterways of Houston, and as you paddle along, thank Terry Hershey, who made possible both the experience and this guide.

Andrew Sansom

Preface

"WHERE DO YOU GO?" is the most frequent question I am asked when I mention canoeing or kayaking. I hope this book will answer that question and encourage readers to come and see for themselves the miles and miles of paddleable waterways all around Houston. It certainly deserves its nickname of "Bayou City"; and there are plenty of lakes, rivers, creeks, bays, and the Gulf of Mexico to paddle when the supply of bayous has been exhausted.

In addition to a constant supply of water, the Houston area is blessed with a climate that allows paddling opportunities year-round. Of course, we don't want to paddle into an approaching hurricane; days with high wind and thunderstorm activity are to be avoided, too, but it is never too hot or too cold to keep us off the water for any length of time.

The availability of relatively inexpensive plastic boats has made kayaking more affordable. Canoes seem to be less popular but are very efficient means of getting out on the water and can typically carry more gear and larger coolers than kayaks. They both have their place. Roof racks, both those provided by automobile manufacturers and those purchased separately, make it easy to carry these boats on the family sedan as well as SUVs and about any other kind of personal transportation.

This guide is intended for both novice and experienced paddlers, canoeists and kayakers. There is always one more place that calls for exploration, and the places we paddle change constantly. I have drawn from many sources for this guide. No one of us knows it all, and as I am writing and looking at maps, I see a continually expanding list of places I want to explore. It is gratifying that a number of organizations in and around Houston are taking up the case for maintaining natural waterways and making them more inviting and accessible. The Bayou Preservation Association comes immediately to mind, as well as the Buffalo Bayou Coalition, the Spring Creek Greenway, the Highland Bayou Quest, and Clear Creek Environmental Foundation, for example.

This guide outlines more than 1,500 miles of paddleable waterways in the Houston area. Of that total, I have personally paddled 500-plus miles in thirty years. At that rate, it looks like I will have plenty to keep me busy exploring waterways for at least the next ninety years. I hope you will enjoy paddling the Houston waterways as much as I have. There is so much to see and do—let's go!

Acknowledgments

MY FIRST PADDLING EXPERIENCES were in Pennsylvania in the early 1970s, first as a member of the Pennsylvania State University Outing Club, then Philadelphia Canoe Club, East Tennessee Whitewater Club, and, after 1982, Houston Canoe Club, Houston Association of Sea Kayakers, Bay Area Council, Boy Scouts of America, and Girl Scouts of South Texas (now merged with the San Jacinto Council). I am a long-standing member of the American Canoe Association and have learned a great deal from club activities and from a multitude of friends. I particularly wish to thank John Sweet and Dave Kurtz for mentoring and encouraging my start in whitewater canoeing and kayaking, including hand construction of the first several kayaks that I paddled. After I moved to Houston, many paddlers introduced me to local paddle trails and those farther away. Anne and Barry Bennick were early guides. Barry's remark that "someday I'm going to write a book about this" started me thinking along those lines. His written guides were a great starting point for this one.

My late boss of twenty-five years, James M. McCloy, proofread the text and made valuable suggestions for improvement.

Many other Houston Canoe Club members have been guides and, equally helpful, willing "guinea pigs" on exploratory trips when I admittedly didn't know where I was going and wasn't sure what I would find when I got there. Marilyn Kircus is the standout good sport in that respect, an inveterate shutterbug, and always willing to head out into the "unknown." John and James Diehl were the first to get me out on the Houston waterways. John and Cindy Bartos, Bob Arthur, Louis Aulbach, Joe Coker, Anne and John Olden, John Ohrt, Ann Derby, Mary Carter, Dana Enos, Dave Kitson, Bill and Donna Grimes, Tracy Caldwell, Chris Kuhlman, Robert Stark, Rob and Paula Kingsbury, Jan Culbertson, Chet and Lillian Tigard, Anneliese Unterharnscheidt, Rudy Rivers, Ron Nunnally, Mary Zaborowski, and Paul Woodcock have all been encouragement, participants, and/or trip leaders who have made a difference for me. If your name isn't here, the omission is inadvertent. You know who you are, and thanks for being there for me.

Friends who make up the canoe training staff for the former South Texas Girl Scout Council put their time and effort where their hearts are in helping girls learn to properly, and safely, enjoy the sport of canoeing. I learned a great deal from them, both in the technique of teaching canoeing and in their dedication to the girls. Linda Brixey, Marsha Hart, Debbie Carey Cooper, Tim Cooper, Lynne Ball, Jonathan Mehta, Rick Gordon, Ron Lindsey, Caasi and Tari Moore, Katie Stallings—you are a special group of people.

I grew up in a family of outdoorspeople. That includes my parents, Hiram and Susanne Wiest; my brothers, Edwin, Randall, John, and Samuel; and my daughters, Ellen Shipman and Susanne Plaisted. Ellen is my uncomplaining and eager-to-go canoeing partner. Mental handicap is no barrier to her canoeing enjoyment. Susanne is perhaps more reluctant, but I hope she will learn to enjoy the natural world around her as Ellen certainly does.

Since I haven't been able to paddle all these miles myself, I often rely on others' reports for information. Eric Ruckstuhl's guides at the Bayou Preservation Association Web site have been particularly helpful. Many trip reports and write-ups are on the Houston Canoe Club's Web site in its newsletter, *WaterLine*.

Unless otherwise noted, photographs were taken by the author. Marilyn Kircus contributed the next-largest number of photos. Sharon Anderson, John Bartos, Bruce Bodson, Joe Coker, and Brad Valtierra furnished other photos. I used a variety of cameras for my photos, all of the "point-and-shoot" variety. The oldest ones were taken with a Pentax Optio WP through about 2005 when the camera met an untimely end in a collision with a rock. It was replaced by an HP digital camera (about 5 MP); and since May 2009 I have used an Olympus Stylus Tough 6000 (10 MP). Canoeing and kayaking are very hard on cameras because of the combination of heat, humidity, water, and hard surfaces. The Olympus and Pentax are "waterproof," but the HP seems to hold its own and cost about half what the other two did.

(Photo by Marilyn Kircus)

Canoeing and Kayaking Houston Waterways

Introduction

HOUSTON'S SUBTROPICAL, HUMID CLIMATE is blessed on average with 50 inches of annual rainfall. This well-watered, generally flat area has many bodies of water that are continuously available for paddling any month of the year. Public parks and boater access points make it legal and easy to float a canoe or kayak but are often unknown outside their immediate geographic area. This guide is meant to acquaint you with places to go paddling, in the hope of retaining our watery natural areas as places of recreation, relaxation, and enjoyment for the Houstonians and area residents who are here now and yet to come.

The guide started with the idea of reviewing the area within 75 miles of downtown Houston. It has expanded somewhat beyond that limit to include larger segments of the Brazos and Colorado rivers that seem logically to fit. It is slightly more abbreviated to our east, where I feel existing river guides have done a nice job of describing the Neches and Angelina rivers, Village Creek, and their tributaries in the Big Thicket area. For areas right on the coast of the Gulf of Mexico and around Galveston Bay, the Texas General Land Office has prepared an excellent *Texas Beach and Bay Access Guide* that is very complete in its information, available at www.glo.state.tx.us/coastal/access/index.html. John Whorff's *Kayaking the Texas Coast* is an excellent guide to the coastline. I concentrate on more inland areas and places I believe are less known but particularly desirable for human-powered craft.

Even though I have lived here thirty years, the "flat-as-a-pancake" topography amazes me. The elevations in the city limits of Houston are no higher than 90 feet above sea level, 50 miles inland from the Gulf of Mexico. Tropical weather events have repeatedly demonstrated that there is no place for heavy rainfall to run off, and the lowest areas flood again and again.

That is the bad side of high rainfall and little elevation change; the good side is that our creeks, rivers, and bayous have enough water to paddle every month of the year—not every creek in every month, but enough that there is always a paddling site available.

The Natural World

One does not have to look far from the asphalt and cement of downtown Houston to see a lush and green natural world. Buffalo Bayou, flowing right through the middle of the city, is paddleable and appealing for its natural beauty as well as for a different view of city life and architecture. Our region is ecologically diverse, from the Post Oak Savannah of the northern parts, to the coastal beaches on the south. The original savannah's native range grasses have degraded from overgrazing, clearing to plant monocultures of "improved grasses," and expanding suburbs. The Coastal Prairie has likewise seen huge losses; in the 1800s the area was used for large cattle grazing operations and, to the southwest, cotton and sugarcane production. Invasive tallow trees were introduced in the mid-1900s, so the prairies now are vastly different from the tallgrass prairies that Native Americans or early European settlers observed.

Wetlands are another important natural feature of our area. With the recent ravages of Hurricanes Katrina, Rita, and Ike, we know that one important effect of wetlands is dampening the destructive forces of storms as they move from the Gulf over the land. Wetlands filter water coming from the land to the sea, and vice versa. They are important nurseries for fish, crabs, and other shellfish and support hunting, fishing, and birding opportunities. They also act as natural detention areas in a spongelike fashion to slow the effects of heavy rainfall and flooding events.

A huge variety of bird species pass through on a seasonal basis or are here year-round. The Great Texas Coastal Birding Trail map to the Upper Texas Coast is highly recommended for locating the best spots to see many of the more than six hundred varieties of birds in Texas each year. On any paddling adventure it is common to see at least one great blue heron, an American egret, and often the snowy egret. Bright pink roseate spoonbills are a special treat, as are reddish egrets, kingfishers, little blue and little green herons, or ospreys. The more you look, the more you see.

There are plenty of reptiles about as well. Many of the most common poisonous snakes of Texas live in our area, among them water moccasins, copperheads, rattlesnakes, and coral snakes. I have seen all but the coral snake from my boat, including one determined rattlesnake swimming across Galveston Bay in front of a host of sea kayakers. We followed at a very respectful distance with occasional glimpses of the rattles on its tail. I wondered whose boatshed it was headed for and was glad it wasn't mine.

The cold-blooded critter that gets everyone's attention is the alligator. You should expect that any body of water large enough to support an alligator probably does, and there are *lots* of them in larger bodies of water. So, in twenty-five years of paddling around Houston, how many times have I been approached by an aggressive alligator? None. I have seen defensive displays, but always because I had inadvertently gotten too close. I remember particularly well a night paddling trip on Armand Bayou. Deeply engrossed in conversation with a fellow paddler, I didn't realize I had pinned an alligator in shallow water up against a steep bank only 10 feet away. This is the first and only (so far) time I have been close enough to have one open its mouth and hiss at me. I assure you, I didn't lose any time in putting some distance between the gator and myself. This is not to say aggressive alligators are not out there or that they will never harm you.

If you are paddling with a pet, you should also know that to an alligator, your pet is a tasty meal. Even 100-pound Labrador retrievers are no match for an alligator, so be very careful where you encourage a dog

Alligator habitat sign in Memorial Park

to jump into the water. Dogs should never be allowed to approach an alligator on land. The sign in the photo is right along Buffalo Bayou in Memorial Park within the city limits of Houston.

Alligators look a lot like floating logs in the water. Most often, all you see of them is the bumps of their eyes and nostrils above water. They sink noiselessly from sight when they hear you coming and often are not seen at all if you are paddling with a large and talkative group. As cold-blooded creatures, alligators cannot control their own body temperatures and must use the warmth of the sun for energy. They try to maintain a steady 89-degree body temperature and feed only when their body is warm enough to digest food. If an alligator feeds when it has a low body temperature, the food cannot be digested; it will spoil in the stomach and possibly kill the alligator. You probably won't want to try to take the alligator's body temperature to decide whether it is feeding today or not. Being cold-blooded makes alligators incredibly efficient at utilizing their food; they need about one-tenth the amount of food to maintain them as warm-blooded animals of the same size. They eat a wide variety of prey—just about anything that moves and is not fast enough to get away. Keep your distance, and do not feed or harass them.

Alligator mating season begins in late March and lasts until the end of May. The mating call is a deep bellow that sounds a lot like a bullfrog's. One of my favorite memories of a canoe trip to Louisiana was paddling the swamps with a group of Cajuns spotting alligators with strong flashlights in the moonlight. Now there's a sport, and an eye-opening experience to how many alligators there are in the water! We could hear their bellows as well as see the gleam in their eyes. In June the females build nests to lay eggs. Mama will stay close by to guard the nest, so it is not a good time to explore that heap of grass and mud near the bayou. The babies hatch around the end of August. Mama is still close and locates them by their chirping sounds. Only about 4 percent survive to adulthood, but the survivors can expect to live twenty-five to thirty years.

Is the Water Safe?

For paddlers, there are several ways to consider water safety: Is the water safe to drink? Is it safe to paddle on? Is it safe for swimming? Can I eat fish or crabs I catch from my boat? In the Houston area it is safe to say no to the first question—you certainly don't want to drink untreated water from any of the water bodies.

Safety for boating recreation has several interpretations. From a whitewater standpoint, we are rather safe; there is hardly a ripple that qualifies as whitewater in our area. There are, however, dams and trees and other obstructions in the water, so read the water carefully and avoid the hazards. Chemical spills and other toxins can contaminate water. When in doubt, don't paddle. Other boats, particularly those with motors capable of high speed, present a real danger to paddlers if operated in a careless manner.

The US Geological Survey (USGS) has gaging stations in many locations on the paddle trails described in this book. Their very useful tables of "Real-Time Water Data for Texas" are available at http://waterdata .usgs.gov/tx/nwis/rt. The National Weather Service's

An alligator sunning at Armand Bayou

Advanced Hydrologic Prediction Service is available at a newer Web site that is particularly helpful in assessing water levels: www.nws.noaa.gov/oh/ahps/. It combines weather predictions with river stages and includes a lot of information about flood stages. My general observation as a paddler, however, is that what the National Weather Service considers an "action level" is generally well out of the safe range for canoeing. Every chapter in this book includes a list of mileages and amenities, as well as the USGS gaging station numbers for the segments of streams in this book. The Harris County Flood Control District has even more monitoring stations and some Web cams on selected parts of the bayous and streams. Many of their gages don't click in until flooding stages are detected.

Swimming safety is generally determined in terms of presence of certain bacteria, particularly *Escherichia coli*. Per the Houston-Galveston Area Council (H-GAC) Clean Rivers Program, nearly half the stream segments covered by this guide are impaired with high bacteria levels. More than 280 sites are monitored through the Clean Rivers Program. Swimming in any of the water bodies in this guide is not recommended. Please refer to the publications of the H-GAC and its monitoring sites to make your own decisions. Remember that even the cleanest waters in our area harbor alligators—think of that before you jump in.

Very few waters are clear enough to see the bottom. Banks along bayous and rivers are notoriously steep, and you can easily slip into very deep water right next to the bank. Clay soils can be incredibly muddy, sticky, and soft, and quicksand occurs along rivers and in wetland areas. Be careful where you walk.

Water temperature is a safety factor. Many areas of the country have very cold, or even frozen, water that presents an immediate danger of hypothermia from immersion. Most of the year this is not a big problem for the Texas Gulf Coast area, but be cautious if you are heading out in the coolest months of the year. Always carry an extra set of dry, warm clothes in a waterproof container. If you paddle long enough, sooner or later you will turn a boat upside down and go for an unintended swim.

This book is not intended as a fishing guide; the safety of eating fish or crustaceans is beyond its scope. Consult the local health district or Houston-Galveston Area Council for more information.

Do I Have a Legal Right to Be Here?

Laws defining "navigable waterways" are complex in delineating who has a right to be on or accessing the water. The Texas Parks and Wildlife Department (TPWD) Web site describes these rights or lack thereof: www.tpwd.state.tx.us/publications/nonpwdpubs/water_issues/rivers/navigation/. This book attempts to describe access points where the property is publicly owned or managed. If in doubt, stay out. You do not have the right to cross private property to access the water or to have a picnic or a restroom break. Please respect the property owners. Property ownership may change over time; the author assumes no responsibility to have accurately portrayed any of these access points as your legal right of access.

Some area waterways are known to be off limits to private boaters: the Houston Ship Channel (lower reaches of Buffalo Bayou) is one of them. An area from roughly the Turning Basin to the San Jacinto State Park is designated as a Safety Zone. Personal boaters are also required to maintain a distance from any US Navy ship or from a cruise ship. Please contact the US Coast Guard for details.

Guidelines for Safe Boating

As much fun as paddling is, there are many ways that trips can go wrong. Consider this discussion a starting point only; it is not complete.

First, recognize that not everyone on the planet is trustworthy. Don't leave your valuables in the car—leave them at home or take them with you on the water in a waterproof container that is made fast to the boat. Number one on your checklist: your car keys. They don't float, and most will rust, or electronics will be destroyed by heat and/or water. How replaceable are your corrective-vision glasses, or sunglasses, or contact lenses? Eyewear should have a safety strap on it, and one that allows eyewear to float when off your head is that much better. We don't intend to turn our boats over when paddling, but it happens often enough.

The hot sun presents another challenge. Hats with a brim are advised (have you tied it on?), for both preventing sunburn and lessening the heat from direct exposure. Next, make sure you have plenty of drinkable water with you. It's easy enough to forget when you are surrounded by water that being next to it does not have the same benefit as having plenty of it in you. The American Council on Exercise recommends drinking before, during, and after exercising. Dehydration headaches (and worse) are fairly common with beginners—make sure you are drinking plenty of liquids. Sugary soft drinks and alcohol do not work as well for hydration as plain unflavored water.

Never paddle alone. As a minimum make sure someone who is not on the trip knows your proposed route, as well as anticipated time for returning. I often carry a cell phone with me, being careful to put it in a waterproof container that is not in the direct sun. Both heat and water are bad business for electronic devices. Not all areas where we paddle have cell phone reception.

Does your skill level match the conditions and route where you are paddling? Most places described in this guide are fairly benign, but high winds and the presence of thunderstorms or other adverse weather can change that in a hurry. Paddling across long reaches of unprotected water (for example, the open bays and lower stretches of the major rivers) makes you particularly vulnerable. Many of our area waterways are tidally affected. Have you checked the high and low tides for the area? What is the water gage reading for the stream you are paddling?

Do you have/need a change of clothing on the trip or at the take-out? Especially in cold weather, a complete extra set of dry clothing (in a waterproof bag, of course) and rain gear are a good precaution. You never know when you might need them; if there is a chance of storm activity, a weather radio is a good source of up-to-date information.

Day-Paddle Checklist

Here is a sample gear checklist to consider for a day trip:

Boat
Paddles (plus one spare paddle per boat)
PFD (personal flotation device or life jacket): There must be one per person. It must be worn by children under twelve and is required to be worn by all participants on club activities. It is highly recommended for everyone to wear at all times.
Throw line: Handy for towing another boat if needed
Maps in waterproof case
Headlamp or flashlight with extra batteries and bulbs if there's any chance of being out after dark
First-aid kit
Pocketknife
Food: Even if you're planning a short trip, you may need the extra energy.
Drinking water. Plenty of it; minimum of 1 quart per every 2 hours
Sunglasses and sunscreen
Canoe chair/backrest: Low-slung "beach chairs" can be nice for a third person riding in a canoe; also nice for lunch breaks. Tie the chair into the boat.
Bailer and large sponge for bailing: A "bailer" is a scooping device to remove quantities of water from the boat, if needed. A plastic bottle with a cap on it, but bottom cut out, works very well. I almost always have a sponge—really nice for cleaning mud out of the boat before inverting it on your clean car.
Waterproof containers for maps, cell phones, extra changes of clothes
Duct tape: Who could live without this on an extended trip? I've used this more than once to paddle out from a remote location when I put a hole in my boat. Yes, I've done this even on the "no rocks" Gulf Coast. Needs to be applied to a dry surface.
Quick-drying pants/shorts/shirt: Cotton takes almost forever to dry, or at least it seems that way on a cold day. Nylon dries out more quickly and is a good wind barrier.

Sun hat with brim: If you can tie it on, so much the better for those windy days.

Bandana: Can be used for cooling when dipped in water and tied around neck; as sunscreen for back of neck, sweatband on a hot day, spill cleanup

Waterproof jacket and pants

Waterproof sandals or booties or old shoes you don't mind getting wet: Getting shoes wet and muddy is a near certainty on most trips. I personally dislike sandals—they provide little or no protection to the sides of your feet if you are walking on or around oyster reefs and present too much of your foot surface to biting/stinging fire ants and mosquitoes.

Garbage bag: Leave your lunch or rest spot cleaner than when you got there; take out what you took in.

Binoculars, field guides: Make sure these are waterproof and protected from the sun.

Camera with waterproof case: My "waterproof" camera also has a float attached to it.

Watch that is heat- and water-resistant

Lip balm: I look for the ones with an SPF factor. I have literally burned my lips on paddle trips, even while wearing a broad-brimmed hat.

Mosquito repellent

Toilet paper: Use your trash bag to take out what you took in.

Brush/comb in case you want to look presentable during or after the trip!

Map and itinerary of trip: Include a note on the location of nearby hospital and/or police access just in case. If you have your cell phone and dial 911, could you tell would-be rescuers where to find you?

Prescription medication: Is anyone on this trip allergic to bee stings? What actions would you take? Does anyone else on the trip potentially need emergency treatment for a medical condition? If you are carrying your medication, make sure it is in a waterproof, secure container with original labeling.

Aspirin and antihistamine: Anyone who carries this should be able to self-administer. There are folks out there who are allergic or otherwise should not take these medications; if you need it, carry it. If you carry it and someone else needs it, think twice before you administer. This applies to sunscreen, too. With Girl Scouts, only trained first aiders can administer to participants whose medical release is signed in advance and carried on the trip. The same applies for ibuprofen and any other over-the-counter medication.

Cell phone: in a waterproof container, out of direct sun

What Boat to Float?

A variety of craft are suitable for paddling around Houston. On the winter outing shown in the photograph, the Houston Canoe Club used canoes and kayaks, singles and tandems.

The first decision is whether to use a canoe or a kayak. There is no single right choice for everyone. I own both kinds of boats and several variants of each. What I paddle depends on the weather conditions, the water body, the duration of the trip, and who is going with me, in the same boat or other boats. I will include the whitewater specialty kayak as a point of reference

A winter's trip with Houston Canoe Club appears to have the paddlers as confused about which direction to point their boats as which craft to paddle. Canoes and kayaks of several persuasions are represented. Photo by John Bartos

although I don't recommend it if you plan to paddle Houston area water exclusively. Of course, there's nothing to stop you from using this craft in the local waters, but I believe you will find it rather inefficient at paddling distances. If that's what you have, paddle it.

There is almost as wide a variety of boat-construction materials as there are types of boats. Since I began paddling in the 1960s, more and more plastics have been developed that have lowered the cost of construction. The lightest boats per model tend to be more expensive; getting light weight and durability is an interesting and sometimes very costly challenge.

Manufacturers offer many models of boats, and there are far more manufacturers than I list here, so be sure to look around. Surf the Web; then see if you can find a local distributor, or visit the local distributor first and refer back to the Web for comparisons. Several of our local canoe/kayak shops will have "demo days" when you can try a variety of craft. There is really no substitute for trying a boat on the water. I present these makes and models of boats for example only; this does not constitute an endorsement or a condemnation of any make or model. The "carrying capacity" weight includes both the weight of the paddler(s) and all the gear in the boat.

Canoes

This fine touring canoe is made for two paddlers. The unusual-looking thwart in the middle is a carrying yoke. It is placed at about the balance point for this canoe so one person can carry it on the shoulders. Notice its relative weight compared to length. At 80 pounds this is no lightweight, but it is very durable.

Whitewater Kayaks

This kayak is made for doing acrobatic stunts and playing on waves in rivers. It is very short so spins easily, which can be very annoying if you are paddling a long stretch of flatwater or trying to keep up with boats that track well in a straight line. It is not designed to carry much, if any, gear.

Whitewater kayak: Riot Magnum, top and side

Decked or Sit-in Recreational Kayak

This kayak will give you a drier ride than the sit-on-top (described next) because you sit in it and the deck of the boat covers at least part of your legs. The sit-in kayak is a lot more stable than a touring kayak and tracks better than a whitewater kayak. It is an inexpensive way to get into paddling but not the most efficient for distance paddling. It is nice for poking along and stable for photography relative to most touring boats.

Sit-on-Top Recreational Kayak

Every double-bladed (kayak) paddle drips water from the upper blade as the lower blade is in the water

Canoe: Old Town Charles River, top and side

Recreational kayak: Perception Prodigy, top and side

Most of the year in Houston the temperature is quite warm, so dripping water on your legs with every stroke isn't a problem—you won't be paddling dry in this boat. The great advantage of a sit-on-top kayak is stability and the freedom for the paddler to move around in the boat. This is a very popular style for fishers. It allows you to paddle into the shallows to get to the best fishing spots and does not have a motor that conks out (you hope, since you are it), make a lot of noise, or reek of gasoline. You can get complete fishing rigs for these kayaks, and there are clubs in the area that will help you improve your skills and offer trips to popular fishing sites.

Recreational kayak, sit-on-top: Ocean Kayak Prowler 13

A sit-on-top kayak outfitted for fishing. This member of the Paddling Anglers in Canoes and Kayaks (PACK) perfectly illustrates the utility of these boats and their incredible stability for practically all positions. Photo by Brad Valtierra

Touring Sea Kayak

Touring Sea Kayak

Sea kayaks are designed to handle wind and waves and paddling distances in a straight line. In general they are more efficient over distance, but they are tippier than other kayaks and canoes illustrated previously. Some models can carry gear for weekend or longer camping trips. Note the rudder for directional stability.

Touring kayak (sea kayak): Current Design Solstice GT, top and side

Paddles

Paddles vary as much as boats do. Contrary to popular opinion, double-bladed paddles can be used in either canoes or kayaks, and single blades can propel a kayak as they do a canoe. A single-bladed traditional canoe paddle won't be as likely to be twisted in low-hanging tree limbs, and you'll stay a lot drier with fewer overhead paddle drips. The kayak paddle seems to be easier for many novice paddlers because it balances strokes more easily. You may, however, discover one arm is much stronger than the other, so don't expect that having the two blades necessarily means you will go in a straight line! This book does not cover technique, but I strongly advise you take some lessons before you set out on a long trip or in challenging weather conditions.

Organization of the Guide

This guide is organized by geography, moving from east to west and north to south. Each of the major river systems and coastal basins is discussed in its own chapter. Many water bodies empty directly into the bays or the Gulf of Mexico, so those are organized by coastal "basin" or the area between lands drained by rivers. Only selected access points for Galveston Island, Galveston Bay, and the Gulf of Mexico coastline are covered. There are simply too many to describe in detail, and they are covered very well by the Texas General Land Office's *Texas Beach and Bay Access Guide* on the Web and in paper format. The Gulf Intracoastal Waterway (ICW) runs through our area, too, and is described in much greater detail in various commercial guides specific to that waterway.

This guide covers a total of 1,500 miles of paddle-able waterways. Of those, I have paddled at least 400 myself. I am relying on other paddlers' reports for some of the other waterways, and for quite a few I can only conjecture mileages and conditions, but they seem likely to be paddleable and desirable. Why don't you try them out and let me know?

Inland waterways are less well known and are the focus of this guide. For an overall view of the waterways discussed in this guide, see the general map at the end of the introduction.

Paddler's Vocabulary

The following terminology and abbreviations are used throughout the book.

Class I Rapids: This is part of an international rating scale for difficulty of moving water from a canoeist, kayaker, or rafter perspective. This is the lowest ranking and defined on the American Whitewater Web site (www.amerianwhitewater.org/content/Wiki/safety:start) as "fast moving water with riffles and small waves. Few obstructions, all obvious and easily missed with little training. Risk to swimmers is slight; self-rescue is easy."

Class II Rapids: This is the next more difficult level of moving water: "Straightforward rapids with wide, clear channels which are evident without scouting. Occasional maneuvering may be required, but rocks and medium-sized waves are easily missed by trained paddlers. Swimmers are seldom injured and group assistance, while helpful, is seldom needed. Rapids that are at the upper end of this difficulty range are designated 'Class II+.'" With the exception of Hidalgo Falls, I am unaware of any water in

our area that is Class II, although any water body that is in flood should be considered dangerous and is not advised for paddling.

Eddy: The fluid dynamics definition is "the swirling of a fluid and the reverse current created when the fluid flows past an obstacle. The moving fluid creates a space devoid of downstream-flowing fluid on the downstream side of the object." Most of the eddies encountered in our area are slow moving; an example would be the upstream flow of water behind the support structures of a bridge.

Eddy out: This applies to moving waters, where one may purposefully pull into an eddy current to take a break from the downstream flow of the main current.

GPS: Global positioning system. Among paddlers the usual application is a handheld device that receives signals from navigation satellites that fix the device's location. These often come with built-in maps and are very useful in determining one's exact location and, if so programmed, the best track to take to reach a certain destination.

ICW: Intracoastal Waterway. An artificial dredged waterway created and maintained by the US Army Corps of Engineers as an aid to waterborne commerce. Its course typically is inland of bays and barrier islands that help protect it from offshore sediment; it also cuts directly across Galveston Bay.

LCRA: Lower Colorado River Authority. A not-for-profit public utility organization that provides services that include electricity, water, flood management, water and wastewater utilities, and public parks along the Colorado River.

PFD: Personal flotation device. Often referred to as a "life jacket" or a "life preserver," this is worn on the person to help keep the person above water in case of voluntary or involuntary immersion.

Put-in: A location where you put your boat in the water, that is, the beginning point of a canoe or kayak trip.

Riffle: A small rapid created by current flowing over typically shallow obstructions.

Beginner's Sampler of Places to Paddle

If you are just getting started with this sport and would like some destinations that are user-friendly and can give you an idea of whether or not you will like paddling, here are some places I recommend as samplers. All have easy, public access to the water and are short paddles for a few hours of relaxation.

1. Armand Bayou: Use the put-in at Bay Area Park.

2. Champion Lake: Not recommended at low-water times or during waterfowl hunting season, although it is closed to hunting for weekend afternoons.

3. Lake Charlotte: Use the access at Cedar Hill Park, and find your way into Mac Bayou, up to Mac Lake. There is water here at almost every season of the year. Winds in excess of 10 miles per hour prohibit a leisurely paddle.

4. Oyster Creek: This is a several-hour float from Brazosport College to Stratton Ridge Road; paddle Stratton Ridge put-in to Oyster Creek Municipal Park; or put in at any of these places and paddle upstream, then back to the boat ramp.

5. Double Bayou: Put in at Double Bayou Park and run the shuttle to Beason Park or paddle up- and downstream from Double Bayou Park.

6. Clear Creek: Put in at Countryside Park; paddle upstream and back to the launch site.

7. Colorado River Columbus Loop: This is a little farther afield but always a pleasant paddle. It requires just a little bit of maneuvering with riffles you may wish to scout before running.

8. Picketts Bayou: See a part of the Trinity River National Wildlife Refuge by paddling out and back along this wooded bayou.

Beginning paddlers will find a 2- to 3-mile trip plenty of exercise for a first-time outing. A paddle of 5 to 8 miles might be considered a moderate workout; 8 miles or more make a good workout for an experienced paddler.

A list of businesses and organizations that may help you get on the water, through sales, instruction, and/or rentals, can be found in the appendix.

River left: The left bank of the river, determined by the direction of flow downriver. This is frequently open to interpretation; be sure to have an agreement with fellow paddlers on how they define river left or river right.

River right: The right bank of the river, determined by the direction of the flow downriver. Like "river left" this may be subject to interpretation by your fellow paddlers—make sure you are in agreement.

Shuttle: For trips that do not return to the same spot where they started, a method of having a pickup (not the vehicle, but a method of getting one's equipment and self picked up) at the end of the trip. Either in advance of the process of unloading at the put-in or after all material has been dropped off at the put-in, leave one or more vehicles at the proposed take-out spot and return in one vehicle to the put-in.

Sit-on-top: A type of kayak in which the paddler sits in the boat without having a deck covering the legs and feet.

Strainer: A tree or other obstruction hanging into the water so that a "comb" effect takes place on large objects, for instance, your canoe or kayak, that try to pass through it.

Sweep boat: The last boat in a group. The typical assignment of a sweep boat is to make sure all members of the trip stay ahead of it and to define the point at which all boats have completed the trip.

Take-out: A place where paddlers take their boat out of the water, that is, the end point of a trip.

TPWD: Texas Parks and Wildlife Department.

USACE: US Army Corps of Engineers.

USGS: US Geological Survey. USGS operates many useful gages that measure the flow rate of rivers and streams and apparent levels of selected lakes.

Notes on Maps

As I set out exploring new places around Houston for paddling trips, I learned some fast lessons on map availability and accuracy. Houston and the surrounding area are growing so fast that obtaining accurate maps that show all the county roads as well as the main thoroughfares and water features is a challenge. The map guides published by Key are quite good for the counties they cover. Online mapping sources such as Topozone (www.topozone.com), Google Earth (www.earth.google.com), and MapQuest (www.mapquest.com) stop short of full utility. Satellite images and aerial photography are great if they are very recent, but it is often up to the viewer to figure out the route names and numbers for land transportation. Much more difficult is a listing of where the rivers are accessible to boaters. If you are searching for a coastal put-in, the Texas General Land Office's Texas Beach and Bay Access Guide is available online. Ron Smith of TPWD has generously allowed me to use the department's inland waters data for this book. Most of the information has not been posted to the TPWD Web site as of the date I am writing this book. Jerry Moulden of Shoreline Publishing created the maps for this book thanks to generous grants from the Bayou Fund and the Bayou Preservation Association. DO NOT USE THESE MAPS FOR NAVIGATION PURPOSES.

I have enjoyed "scouting" several of these waterways via Google Earth, which is evolving as we speak, and through Microsoft's earth imaging software. I am amazed as I follow the maps at how well sandbars show up on remote rivers, and one can even count the number of cars in parking lots. It's not nearly as much fun as actually paddling but gives a much better idea of what you might be in for than anything available in the past.

Overview of waterways

1
East Bay, Eastern Trinity Bay, and the Neches-Trinity Coastal Basin

Bolivar Peninsula

BOLIVAR PENINSULA, a narrow strip of land between the East (Galveston) Bay and the Gulf of Mexico, is 27 miles long and at its widest spot only 3 miles wide. It is reached by land only through Chambers County and, on the southwest, via the Bolivar ferry from Galveston Island. From the peninsula you can access the waters of both the bay and Gulf of Mexico. All paddling routes are exposed to wind, weather, current, and tides.

The peninsula took a terrific hit from Hurricane Ike in September 2008. Many homes were completely destroyed to their foundations, beach erosion was severe, and property loss was immense. The Texas General Land Office's *Texas Beach and Bay Access Guide* and many of the fishing maps of the area were excellent before the storm at locating places to put a boat in the water. All of these access points should be double checked for availability post-Ike.

Three trips that may be of interest are putting in from the beach next to the ferry landing and paddling the bay side of the peninsula, or the ICW, to Stingaree Marina (and having a fried seafood dinner to reward your paddling effort); from Stingaree Marina to Rollover Pass; and from Rollover Pass across the bay to Oyster Bayou and back. From here you will find the bayside pretty much unspoiled by human habitation with some lovely sand beaches all to yourself and the occasional fishers.

East Bay

East Bay is bounded to the south by Bolivar Peninsula and tapers to the east to East Bay Bayou. The ICW parallels the bay's northern shore. Anahuac National Wildlife Refuge (ANWR) is on the northeastern part of the bay.

East Bay Bayou

East Bay Bayou can be accessed from TX 124 boat ramp on the east, and from the ANWR on its East Bay Bayou Tract. This access has a gated entrance road, with limited hours, usually dawn to dusk. Check with the office (409-267-3337) to make sure you don't get locked in and to see if it is currently open. To get to this tract, travel east on FM 1985 past the entrance of the ANWR for another 4 miles and look for the right-hand turn. You will have two choices of places to put a boat in the water: the first right turn off the access road or another half mile farther where the restrooms and public boat launch are located.

East Bay Bayou is draped with live oaks close to the put-in. Oaks give way to open coastal prairie and wetlands closer to the bay. This is pretty much an out-and-back trip unless you want to try making it a 10-mile excursion that includes connecting to the ICW and following it east to 124.

Anahuac National Wildlife Refuge

Directions. To get to the main refuge from I-10 East, take Exit 812 (TX 61, Anahuac/Hankamer). Head south on 61 for nearly 4 miles to the stop sign (1 mile past the new visitor center). Continue straight across the intersection. The road becomes FM 562. Continue for approximately 8.5 miles to the fork in the road at FM 1985. At the fork, turn left on FM 1985 and continue for an additional 4 miles to the main entrance of the refuge. Turn right on the easement road for another 3 miles. Past the on-site visitor center; the second road to the right goes to the Bay Boat Ramp and Overlook (marked Boat Launch on the map). A brand-new visitor center with signage from I-10 is actually on TX 563 (not 562), only 3 miles south of I-10.

0 1 2

1985

Boat
Launch

East Bay
Bayou

124

124
Boat Ramp

Boat Launch

Visitor
Center
(Anahuac NWR)

Oyster
Bayou

High
Island

Robinson
Lake

Robinson
Bayou

Onion
Bayou

Boat
Launch

Intracoastal Waterway

East Galveston Bay

Frozen Point

Marsh Point

Gulf of Mexico

*East
Galveston
Bay*

Bolivar
Peninsula

Rollover Pass

For purposes of this discourse on canoeing and kayaking, I won't go into a detailed description of ANWR, but I encourage you to visit with or without a boat to enjoy one of the best bird-watching areas in the world. Winter avian residents are spectacular for their numbers and variety. Ducks and geese abound. Warmer seasons give the alligators a chance to show off; spring and fall migrations are spectacular for long-distance fliers. There is a brand-new visitor center just off TX 61 about 3 miles south of I-10 (not on the refuge grounds proper). There are wonderful displays, a walking path to Lake Anahuac, and knowledgeable staff to orient you to the area.

Paddling is not allowed on the ponds of the refuge, but there are several access points from the refuge to good paddling destinations. The refuge, its roads, and facilities were severely impacted by Ike. Boat ramps may be accessed, but bay patterns and even the form of the land have changed significantly. Do not count on drinking water being available on the refuge.

Oyster Bayou

Directions. To get to Oyster Bayou, take the first left turn beyond the entry pond and walkway within ANWR. There is a boat ramp on the canal to Oyster Bayou. From that access point, it is an 8- or 10-mile paddle one way to the southernmost tip of ANWR. The bayou itself is large and well defined, but by all means carry a good map and compass when you paddle here; and remember that if you paddle 10 miles downstream, you have to turn around and paddle 10 miles back upstream to return to your vehicles!

My experience with Oyster Bayou came from across East Galveston Bay, putting in at Rollover Pass on the Bolivar Peninsula. This trip took place in August, departing Rollover around 4:00 p.m., returning after dark. We paddled sea kayaks, using both compasses and good maps to test our navigation skills, as the distant shoreline looks rather featureless from miles across the open bay. From the bayou, you will note how incredibly flat this area is, a very large marsh area with few places to get out and stretch your legs and many "Keep Off" signs. A high-and-dry lunch spot may

offer good viewing of alligators cruising for dinner less than 50 feet away.

Robinson Bayou

The Bay Boat Ramp in ANWR is a good access point to Robinson Bayou, a delightful coastal marsh paddle. You should know, however, that the east side of the lower bayou, although it is owned by ANWR, is a closed area; the other banks and the lake are privately owned. You are okay as long as you stay in your boat, but know that everywhere else you are not. This deepwater bayou is paddleable year-round.

Coastal marshes along East Bay Bayou where it joins the open bay waters

The distance to Robinson Lake is about 5 miles via the bayou, but likely 2 or less as the crow flies. You can see on the map how much the bayou twists and turns. Although there are very few trees, the bayou sits down in the coastal prairie and is fairly protected from the wind.

Smith Point, East Galveston Bay, and Eastern Trinity Bay

➡ *Directions.* There are three sites to launch boats at Smith Point. Robbins Park is public (no charge); Spoonbill RV Park is a private site with a fee to park/launch there. The third site is from the parking lot at the observation tower of Candy Abshier Wildlife Management Area. The approach to all is from FM 562, at least 20 miles south of I-10 East. Robbins Park and Spoonbill RV Park are accessed from Hawkins Camp Road, your last available right turn from Smith Point

Road (FM 562, Smith Point Road). The decision point for Spoonbill or Robbins Park is on Hawkins Camp Road 1.3 miles from the turnoff from FM 562. Go right for Spoonbill or left for Robbins. There are full facilities, including a campground for RVs at Spoonbill; there are only a dirt parking lot and paved boat ramp at Robbins. For the Abshier WMA lot, go left from FM 562 at the WMA sign. There is a wonderful bird observation tower and a large paved parking lot with access to East Galveston Bay. For access and accommodation information at Spoonbill RV Park, call 409-355-2347.

On a January trip from Smith Point, Spoonbill RV Park, I had some interesting weather challenges. Across the bay to the west and north were large, dark, menacing clouds that had obviously drenched Smith Point earlier. Several miles into the trip thunder rumbled and rain showers blew around us. At one point, a herd of cattle thought we might be their ticket to safety

Chris Kuhlman and the author enjoying a winter's solstice kayak trip on Robinson Bayou. Photo by Marilyn Kircus

Eastern Trinity Bay

and started following us along the shore. With the thunder and dark clouds on the horizon, we debated turning around and what our best choice was if the storm came our way, but in the end we kept paddling. We encountered only heavy drizzle before the clouds headed away from us, and the day warmed and brightened as the storm continued on its route westward. Back at home in League City, my rain gauge measured 3 inches of rainfall.

Once we passed Frankland Point, there were very few houses until we reached Oak Island and Beason Park. Brown pelicans dived on the waters; several shell beaches evidenced the presence of earlier Native Americans who camped, fished, and clammed this area at least two hundred years ago. More such middens have been found many miles farther south but are now covered with water. On this day, the kayakers were the only ones on the water.

Lone Oak Bayou

Lone Oak Bayou drains a good-sized coastal marsh about halfway between Oak Island and Smith Point.

One of several shell middens along the east shore of Galveston Bay

I have seen small fishing boats going into the water where the bayou goes under FM 562. It appears to be about 4 miles in length as it meanders to its mouth on Trinity Bay.

Double Bayou

Directions. Double Bayou drains an area of 100 square miles. It is paddleable year-round. The East Fork is about 28 miles in total length, and the West Fork about 15 miles; typically, only the lower 6 or so miles of each fork are paddled. Good public access points are at Double Bayou Park and Job Beason Park. Double Bayou Park is about 5.5 miles from Job Beason Park, just downstream of where the East Fork and West Fork merge. Beason Park is a popular launching place for trailered fishing boats, so expect a lot of activity near its boat ramp. Usually people are fishing and picnicking along the bulkheaded bank of the bayou. To get to Beason Park from Double Bayou Park, go west on Eagle Ferry Road until it dead-ends at FM 563; go left (south on 563) about a mile and a half, watching for the boat ramp signs and the park on your left.

James Jackson settled in the Double Bayou area in 1847, establishing a ranch of 26,000 acres. In 1880 Joshua Harmon operated a cotton gin on the site of present-day Beason Park. Job Beason, for whom the park is named, was the lightkeeper for Double Bayou Lights in the early 1900s. He was found floating facedown in the water in December 1909. When the hurricane of 1915 destroyed the lighthouse, it was not rebuilt. Hurricane Ike in September 2008 devastated the town of Oak Island.

As the name implies, Double Bayou is a two-pronged bayou, with an East Fork and a West Fork that converge very close to their mouth on Galveston Bay at Oak Island. This part of Chambers County is still fairly undisturbed, although the lower end of the West Fork has been dredged for about 3 miles from Oak Island to allow shallow-draft commercial boat traffic, typically barges and shrimp boats. The depth of the natural stream has made it a popular sailing destination for smaller sailboats in the Galveston Bay area, and it isn't unusual to see one or more of them moored several miles upstream even on the natural East Fork bayou. Cattle ranching is the most obvious use of the coastal grasslands along the bayou. Historically there was a lot of rice farming in the area as well, although saltwater flooding from tropical storms wiped out many crops. Much of the stream bank is forested with oaks, elms, gums, and some pine trees, particularly in the upper reaches.

■ *Paddling Note.* Paddling Double Bayou is somewhat of a gambler's choice for routes. Current is typically negligible, so from either park you can travel upstream or downstream and return to your put-in, or paddle one direction only to the other park. A recent Houston Association of Sea Kayakers (HASK) trip put in at Beason Park, paddled upstream to Double Bayou Park for lunch, and paddled back to Beason Park in 5 hours. We were all paddling sea kayaks, which move upstream with relative ease; I would expect the same trip in a canoe to take longer. All of my first experiences on Double Bayou were in canoes. The upper stretches in particular are well protected from the wind by large trees that in some places actually touch across the water. A nice relaxed trip for a family or youth group outing would be paddling from Double Bayou Park down to Beason Park. If the youth have an overabundance of energy for such a short trip, run it in reverse.

Double Bayou Park is wooded. Many of its largest trees were destroyed by Hurricane Ike, but within months the park was cleaned and many new oak trees planted.

An unusual feature of the bayou in the fall is the large number of golden orb weaver spider webs high up where the overhanging trees provide a framework. In September 2004 many belted kingfishers were flying from bank to bank and along the bayou. Little blue herons and osprey were numerous; cardinal flowers flushed red blooms, and pickerelweed bloomed blue.

On a canoe trip several years ago we observed a crab and small snake locked in a deadly embrace. The

Robert Stark paddling upstream in Double Bayou, a deep-draft bayou

crab won this duel, and we paddled on to end the trip with a friendly lunch of beer and burgers in a restaurant overlooking the bayou in Oak Island.

East Shore, Trinity Bay

I have not paddled the stretch between Beason Park and Fort Anahuac to the north. From observation and maps, the Anahuac/Beason stretch goes by fish camps and homes, both Ike survivors and new

construction. The spoil island downstream of Double Bayou's entrance to the bay looks to be the most substantial or perhaps the only island along this stretch until you are within 3 miles of Fort Anahuac Park. Also of interest along this stretch is Round Point, at one time home of Anson Taylor, whose three sons were killed in the Battle of the Alamo, and after that, home to Thomas Jefferson Chambers, for whom Chambers County is named.

For a description of Fort Anahuac Park, see chapter 2.

Well-shaded upper stretches of Double Bayou

*Cardinal flower in
bloom along the banks
of Double Bayou*

Facilities

East Bay, Eastern Trinity Bay, and the Neches-Trinity Coastal Basin

Paddling area	Access point	Toilet	Picnic	Camping	Water	Ramp	Parking	Gage	Mileage	Comments
Bolivar Peninsula										
	Bolivar ferry landing				●		●		15	Beware ferry wake and turbulence
	Stingaree Marina	●				●	●		10	
	Rollover Pass						●			
East Bay										
East Bay Bayou			●			●	●		5	
Anahuac National Wildlife Refuge		●					●			
	Oyster Bayou								10	
	Robinson Bayou								15	
	Anahuac National Wildlife Refuge ramp					●	●			Wildlife viewing area
Smith Point, East Galveston Bay, and Eastern Trinity Bay							●			Observation platform at Candy Abshier Park
Lone Oak Bayou									4	
	FM 562 crossing									
Double Bayou									12	
	Double Bayou Park	●	●			●	●			
	Job Beason Park	●	●			●	●			
East Shore, Trinity Bay									20	

2 Trinity River System

THE ORIGINAL human inhabitants of the lower Trinity River were the Bedias and Orcoquisac peoples. They were hunter-gatherers living off the largesse of the land. Many cultural middens remain as signatures of their occupation. The most obvious middens are of rangia clam shells, a species whose off-flavor was not appealing to Europeans and whose numbers have decreased as their growing areas have increased in salinity. Middens appear all through the lower Trinity River and along the shores of Trinity Bay, and many are now submerged on the continental shelf even miles out from the current Gulf shore.

When René-Robert Cavelier, Sieur de la Salle came to the mouth of the Trinity in 1687, he called it "River of the Canoes," so it would seem entirely appropriate to make this a modern travel destination. Spaniards in Mexico wanted to keep the French at bay in Louisiana and hoped to prevent their encroaching on what today is East Texas by building missions. Without large numbers of émigrés from Spain, the hope of the missions was to convert Native Americans to Christianity and have them take up arms to support the Spanish claims. One such mission, El Orcoquisac, was established in 1756 as the site of a Native American village near present-day Lake Miller. It displaced François Simars de Bellisle's outpost. The mission sat next to the Camino del Bahia trail, which connected through Moss Bluff to Atascocita and to the west to the Camino Real. Exposure to European diseases decimated the Native Americans; bad water from the swampy lake, biting insects, a fire, and tropical hurricanes made life a misery for the Spaniards. They abandoned the mission and presidio in 1771.

The Trinity's watershed covers almost 18,000 square miles in its 715 miles to Galveston Bay. It is a slow-moving river, dammed to form Lake Livingston 120 miles upstream of the bay. Its waters are used for rice field irrigation for most of that stretch, so Livingston dam is discharging throughout the rice-growing season, providing plenty of water for paddling activities. Heavy rainfall events have created major floods in all sections of the river; not even Lake Livingston can hold enough to prevent them. The riverbanks are heavily wooded, and sandbars are common. The backwaters and cypress swamps that drain to the river add to its mystique.

Included in the Trinity complex are its old meander beds, the Old and Lost rivers. Lakes Charlotte, Miller, and Mud are here; and lower still, Cotton Lake and Lake Anahuac. The Trinity is the largest source of freshwater in the Galveston Bay system. The oyster reefs downstream of its mouth are some of the most productive in the bay.

When I first paddled the lower Trinity, one had to be cautious about barge traffic. Historically, barges ran as far as Liberty, and proposals were afoot to make it navigable as far upstream as Dallas. Frequent shoaling and large loads of sediment to feed shifting sandbars made this economically unfeasible. The dynamic atmosphere of the Trinity has made for many "interesting" trips for me, finding to my chagrin that maps and actual navigable waterways are not always in congruence.

The Trinity River Authority created the Trinity River Basin Master Plan in 2001 to manage the Trinity's multiple functions. Recreational uses have not been a top priority, and as stated in the plan, "Mere access to the main stem of the Trinity River is a problem." Many of the access points for the main Trinity are from highway rights-of-way or are informal "ramps" that can be challenging for canoes and kayaks. More developed put-in and take-out locations would certainly be desirable. Some 17,000 acres of bottomland hardwood

24

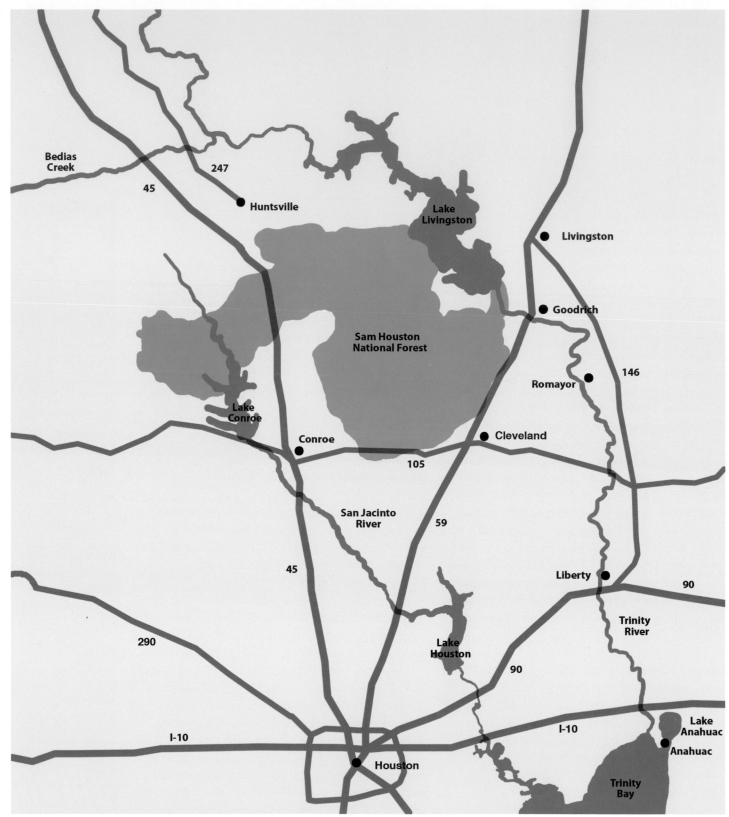

Overview of Trinity River System

forest along the Trinity are being actively acquired for a Trinity River National Wildlife Refuge. The Friends of the Trinity River Refuge group is working with the US Fish and Wildlife Service to preserve and enhance the refuge through conservation, research, and education. The Friends have received not-for-profit 501(c)3 status and serve as the liaison between the refuge and the public.

Interstate 10 crosses the Trinity about 30 miles to the east of downtown Houston. The largest bodies of water you see along this stretch are the Old and Lost rivers and their lakes, followed by the high arching bridge over the Trinity itself. Since the 1960s there has been debate about damming the Trinity in this area; the town of Wallisville was purchased by the US Army Corps of Engineers, and its remaining buildings moved to Wallisville Heritage Park in anticipation of flooding. Public opposition to the dam prevented the final result, replacing plans for a large dam with a much smaller inflatable dam to prevent saltwater intrusion. In 2003 the USACE established the Mayes Wildlife Trace just to the west of the I-10 river crossing. Its scenic drive and outlooks afford great opportunities to view the plants and wildlife of the area. Heritage Park is at Exit 807 off I-10 and is well worth a detour from your shuttle run or river trip. The Wallisville Lake Visitor Center is accessed from the Ranger Station/Visitor Center Access Road, going south from Heritage Park. The visitor center has a museum, a local wildlife display, and a public boat ramp a little farther down the road. I have not used the boat ramp myself, but it looks like a good possibility for paddling down the Trinity (providing the saltwater barrier isn't inflated!) to take out from Hugo Point or even Fort Anahuac Park some miles downstream.

■ *Paddling Note.* Because the Trinity is such an active stream, with frequent flooding, silt deposition, and rechannelization, I quickly learned that published maps of the Trinity are often incorrect. Lower reaches, of course, are tidal as well, so even aerial photography can be deceptive, depending on the water levels. Good gages for the river are maintained by the USGS and other agencies.

The lower reaches are rarely too low for recreational canoeing and kayaking—it's your choice how much mud you want to wade through to get to paddleable water when the river is low. At highest water levels, I have put in from beside the road and paddled right over the top of what at usual levels is dry woodland. I do not recommend paddling at extreme flood stage when the current can be very strong and you can encounter large drifts of tree branches, fire ants, and anything else that might float.

Above Lake Livingston: Bedias Creek

➡ *Directions.* Access to the creek is from the highway right-of-way along FM 247 north and west of Huntsville. Although I-45 and US 75 cross farther to the west, I do not know if the creek has enough water in it to make it navigable the 5 to 8 miles between these two locations. The day I was checking it out was after a record rainfall and a record water level, the highest in forty years. It was certainly navigable that day, if not outright wild and rushing through the woods. Where 45 and 75 cross, there are north and south branches of the creek; the northern one appears to be the larger.

The creek takes its name from the Bidais Native Americans who were agriculturalists and lived in a village where the current Bedias Creek flows into the Trinity River. Their population was never large and was completely decimated by disease and incursions by other Native Americans by the beginning of the nineteenth century.

The *Analysis of Texas Waterways* describes some parts of Bedias Creek as being desirable for recreationists, especially in periods of adequate rainfall. It gives an "interesting" description of a "considerable rapid [that] makes a ten-foot drop over a lineal distance of approximately fifty feet and could be hazardous to the unwary." That would be a major hazard in my book, so be very wary if you are running this stretch—let me know how you navigated it! The creek is lined with oak, elm, willow, and pecan. It is spring fed so supposedly always has a flow.

The put-in/take-out is described as very steep. The creek is known for its white bass fishing, so you may

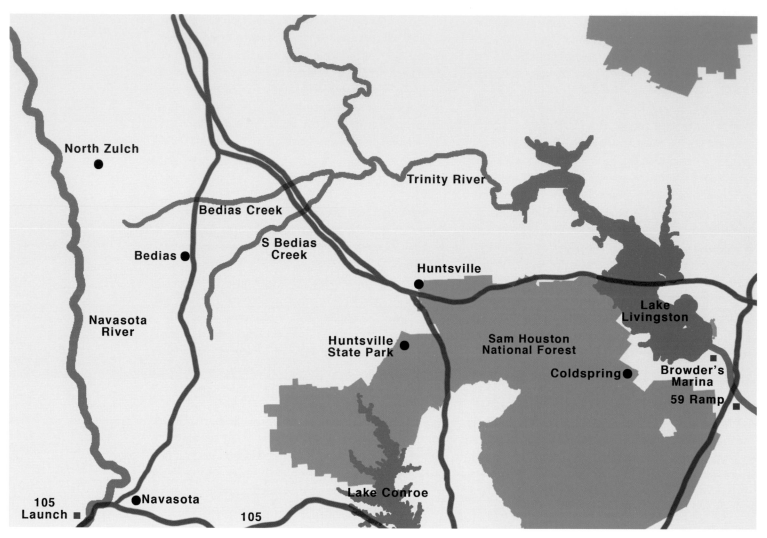

North Zulch

Trinity River

Bedias Creek

S Bedias
Creek

Bedias

Huntsville

Navasota
River

Huntsville
State Park

Lake
Livingston

Sam Houston
National Forest

Coldspring

Browder's
Marina

59 Ramp

Lake Conroe

105
Launch

Navasota

105

Bedias Creek

want to be cautious about being on the stream when the fish are running. Motorcraft travel upstream into Bedias Creek from the Trinity River.

Lake Livingston

Lake Livingston State Park provides access to its namesake lake from several locations in the park. The lake itself covers more than 90,000 acres, so there is plenty of open water to explore, with the usual caveats of the potential for wind, wakes, and high-speed powerboats. The Trinity River Authority (TRA) manages the lake and water releases below the lake into the Trinity River. TRA can be reached for more information at 936-365-2292. TRA also manages Wolf Creek Park with overnight camping and boating access to Lake Livingston. It is open March 1 through November; campsite reservations can be made at 936-653-4312. There are many day-use areas with access to the water.

Double Lake Recreation Area

Also within the upper Trinity River drainage is small 23-acre Double Lake, which offers family camping and a lake very suitable for paddling. For more information, call the National Recreation Reservation Service at 877-444-6777.

Trinity River Access Points

Access 1: Below Lake Livingston Dam

From FM 3278 at the base of Livingston Dam, there are twin access points to the river from both the east and west sides. These launching spots are managed by Browder's Marina, some distance west of the river on 3278. Stop by the office to purchase a pass to use the facilities, drop off a boat, or leave a car. Large signs to that effect are posted at the access roads in case you forget; and in addition to the right to launch and leave a vehicle at these parks, there are facilities with electricity and restrooms available nearby. A large, free, paved boat ramp and parking facility are located 11 miles downstream.

■ *Paddling Note.* Aerial photography of this stretch prior to Hurricanes Katrina and Rita (2005) show huge white sandbars along the upper portion; the upper bars in particular have been considerably eroded and the trees stripped of their leaves, so they were not as spectacular as I had anticipated when I paddled here in October 2006. Huffman and Long King creeks are tributaries. This is a popular stretch (including upstream almost to the dam) with fishers, and you will see them in johnboats and other shallow-draft craft all along here. The waters look deceptively placid and slow moving, but don't be lulled into inattentiveness; there are huge snags that can stop you in your tracks and turn your boat over if you are unwary. Within a quarter mile of the take-out is a "forest" of metal pipes on river right. They can be a very dangerous impediment—be careful and keep your distance.

This segment has beautiful timber along both sides, one fast-moving water segment, and a "wild" feel to it. In a sea kayak I can paddle these 11 miles in 3.5 hours; count on about double that time if you wish to just drift and enjoy the sandbars. An improved ramp on your right is private property of a local community—there are no public access spots along this stretch.

Within view of the US 59 bridge, we sighted a bald eagle at the edge of the river, an unusual bird for our area in general and rumored to be nesting in the vicinity. Expect to see lots of ducks on this segment, which make it desirable to hunters but not to boaters during the waterfowl hunting season.

Access 2: US 59 Crossing

There is a huge concrete boat ramp here and a parking lot. Make sure your brakes are working well before heading down this ramp. It is long and steep enough that you don't want to carry boats from the top to bottom, or more important, bottom to top, but it is an excellent place to get to the river. Access to the ramp is only from the southbound lanes, so if you are northbound, watch carefully for the ramp before you cross the river.

Your next access point downstream is 22 miles farther per the *Analysis of Texas Waterways*. I am told that Menard Creek, which enters the Trinity about 14 miles downstream, is a potential access point for the Trinity; but the place you can put a boat on Menard Creek is 1.5 miles upstream from the Trinity, not a very viable takeout.

Access 3: Menard Creek

➔ *Directions.* To get to the access point for Menard Creek, take TX 146 north from Liberty to the intersection with FM 787. Travel west on 787 toward Romayor, about 5 miles. At Romayor, take FM 2610 approximately 3 miles north to the stream crossing. The best access to the stream is at the northwest corner of the crossing.

This is not a desirable take-out spot because of the required 1.5-mile upstream paddle. It has potential as a put-in, so the downstream current works in your favor, but I have not tried it myself. Paralleling the creek is a hiking trail. It would be worthwhile to hike the trail to look at the creek and decide on its paddleability before launching.

The stream has a lot of logs and debris on it, so paddle with caution. It empties into the Trinity at a broad sandbar. Once you are on the Trinity, it is about 7 miles from this point to the 787 crossing.

▶ *Marilyn Kircus setting off on the Trinity River on a still morning below Lake Livingston dam*

▼ *The Trinity River some miles downstream of the Lake Livingston dam with an overgrown sandbar to the right*

Access 4: FM 787 Crossing

This is an unimproved access to the river from the highway right-of-way. The best access is from the shoulder of the road close to the bridge, with a scramble down the bank and across a sandbar.

From 787 it is 30 miles to the TX 105 crossing. The *Analysis of Texas Waterways* appears to have omitted this stretch, ignoring all mention of the FM 787 crossing, so this distance is my best estimate from the maps I have available. The river meanders considerably and is heavily forested. There is potential for several intermediary access points, but none appear to be on public property.

Access 5: TX 105 Crossing

This is another unimproved access point: there are about 100 yards of riverbank along the highway right-of-way. It is a fairly difficult access point, about 4 miles west of the community of Moss Hill, not to be confused with Moss Bluff many miles farther downstream.

The next access I am aware of is at the US 90 crossing near Liberty. Potential intermediate river access points are at Dayton Lakes and Kenefick, but I haven't tried them and do not know how usable they are, or if they might be considered "in the public domain." The TX 146 bridge is about 30 miles downstream from the 105 bridge. There has been some development reported along the riverbanks, but much of it is in a wild state. Aerial photography shows a mix of woodlands and large sandbars along the river.

Access 6: US 90 Crossing

From the west bank of the river are a good access area, parking, and a boat ramp. When paddling to this ramp from upstream, you will pass under a railroad bridge upstream of the highway bridge.

Access 7: Port Street Boat Ramp

→ *Directions.* This access point is also reached from US 90 and is the property of Texas Parks and Wildlife Department. Heading east from the Trinity River crossing in the town of Liberty, turn right on Navigation Road. A "public boat ramp" sign marks the turn. In about half a mile, turn right on Port Road and

follow it to the ramp. Facilities include a ramp and large paved parking lot.

This access, location of the former Port of Liberty, puts you on a meander neck cutoff of the Trinity River. When the Trinity is light brown with floodwaters, this stretch remains quiet and still. At lower levels, you cannot reach the main body of the Trinity because of a sandbar at its mouth.

Downstream of Liberty, sloughs and marshes increase as you get closer and closer to the coast—there is even an increased wild, primeval feel to this stretch. Tall woodlands with blackwater swamps become numerous, although the riverbed itself is well defined, so you shouldn't get lost—unless you are paddling with me. I always find a way to get lost. Sometimes the maps are completely wrong, thanks to the meanders of the river, its depositing then removing sand and sandbars, and eating away at banks in some places or replacing them with sandbars in others. I have been particularly challenged by the Old and Lost river areas, the Cutoff, and Picketts Bayou, which seems particularly elusive and averse to mapping. If your map shows a wide mouth of Picketts Bayou onto the Trinity, don't believe it—unless it has changed once again from the last time I got lost trying to find it.

From the boat ramp at US 90/TX 146 west of Liberty, it is 28 miles downstream to the I-10 access; there are several potential intermediary stops, but you had better scout them carefully—they won't be easy to spot from the river.

Access 8: Moss Bluff/Picketts Bayou Stretch

→ *Directions.* From FM 563 north of I-10, proceed to the intersection with CR 133 toward Moss Bluff. At the intersection with CR 1333 (Granada Lake Civic Association sign), turn left and follow to the intersection with CR 1334. At that intersection, the Granada Lake Civic Association sign is behind you. Directly ahead is a dirt road that goes over a hump and down to the river, which you can't see from the road. Do not try this when the water is high or there has been a lot of rain.

One of my exploratory trips involved a hunt for

0   1   2

Demijohn Lake

Moss Bluff

Champion Lake

Wooten Lake

1409

Picketts Bayou

Mac Bayou

Old River Cutoff Access

Cedar Hill Park

Winfree

Old River

John Wiggins Bayou

Lake Charlotte

563

Hankamer

Lost Lake

565

Mud Lake

Lake Pass

Lake Miller

Lost River

I-10

Cove

Old River Lake Pu-tin

I 10 Boat Ramp

Wallisville

Wallisville Turtle Bayou Rd

Turtle Bayou

White Memorial Park

Old River Lake

Round Lake

Trinity River

563

Buns Beach

Cotton Lake Boat Ramp

Hugo Point

Trinity River Is Recreational Ctr

Lake Anahuac

Cotton Lake

61   65

Genco Cooling Lake (Off Limits)

562

Anahuac

West Fork Double Bayou

Trinity Bay

Anahuac Park

Lower Trinity River Basin

Picketts Bayou, a prominent feature of the map I had in hand. The first challenge of the day was to find a way to put in on the river, and after consulting with several of the locals, we were pointed to a "customary use" type of boat ramp. Its best description is a dirt road to a dirt ramp on a sandbar that appears to be stable enough at most water levels to support a car. In pursuit of the mouth of Picketts Bayou, paddle upstream. In our search for the bayou, which looked to be an obvious intersection, we paddled and we paddled and found two beautiful bayou openings on the east bank of the Trinity, all black from tannic acid and swamp drainage—but no west bank entrance to Picketts Bayou.

We continued upstream until we were quite sure we had passed the bayou. On the return trip, at the spot on the river where I was sure the bayou had to be, was an overgrown sandbar 4 feet high. I struggled out of my kayak, topped the sandbar—and lo, there was the bayou. It certainly had enough water to float a boat, but also a lot of downed trees and saplings across it, sure to be a bushwhacking trip for who knows what distance. We decided to explore the bayou from another direction another day. The Trinity flows broad and deep here, through upland as well as lowland forests and swamps. Great and snowy egrets were a common sight, with an occasional great blue heron. Spotted sandpipers were numerous.

The author exploring a blackwater bayou emptying into the Trinity River. Photo by Marilyn Kircus

If you decide to use an alternate take-out from Moss Bluff, it is possible to paddle from there 8 miles to Cedar Hill Park via a cut to the Trinity from Mac Bayou and on in to Lake Charlotte. Otherwise, from Moss Bluff to the next takeout on the Trinity is about 12 miles at I-10.

Access 9: I-10 Crossing

There is a public boat ramp on the east side of the river under the I-10 bridge. Use Exit 807 (Wallisville) and follow the access road under the bridge. The next access is 6 miles downstream.

Access 10: Mayes Trace / Trinity River Island Recreation Area

This access is an entrance to the Old River / Lost River / Old River Cutoff complex. Wallisville Heritage Park on the I-10 frontage road has good exhibits about the area, and the Mayes Wildlife Trace entrance is just west of the visitor center. What you need to know about these two access roads is that they are on op-posite sides of the Trinity River, and you cannot cross from one to the other without a boat at the southern termini. The Trace includes boardwalks and wildlife-viewing stations, and its 4-mile access road runs atop the levee on the west bank of the Trinity. The recre-ation area is accessed from I-10, Exit 806 (or 807 if you are coming from the east). It is on the east side of the Trinity and has fishing access, picnic tables, restrooms, a two-lane boat ramp, and a lot of paved parking. There is a lovely bird rookery and viewing station just to the east of the Trinity River bridge on the south side of I-10. It's worth taking a look at the swamp; if you are lucky, you will see thousands of white ibises and other marsh birds on their nests. This area is not open to paddling.

An inflatable dam/saltwater barrier, which you can see at the Trinity River Recreation Area, is the end result of years of litigation and disagreements between conservationists and dam builders in this ecologi-cally sensitive area. The headquarters for the USACE, Wallisville Project, is here as well. Be sure to stop in the visitor center to see the museum and to pick up a map of the Wallisville Lake Project. The next access is 4 miles downstream in Anahuac.

Access 11: Port of Anahuac

The Chambers-Liberty Counties Navigation District maintains the Port of Anahuac at the base of Lake Anahuac along the Trinity River at the foot of Miller Street and Bolivar Avenue. By lifting and car-rying your canoe or kayak across the dam (not a tall one; this is very doable), you can put your boat on Lake Anahuac. Or you can drive to a canoe and kayak access area on the south end of Lake Anahuac at North Main Street. If you would like to take advan-tage of prevailing southerly winds during the summer, it's fun to try rigging a sail and sailing and paddling across the lake to the Turtle Bayou access point to the north. Do run a shuttle—it's not nearly so much fun to paddle back into the wind if you have left a car at the south end only.

Access 12: Fort Anahuac Park

➜ *Directions.* Fort Anahuac Park is about 1 mile downstream from the Port of Anahuac. To reach the park, take I-10 to Exit 812 (TX 61, Hankamer, and Anahuac). Follow 61 south about 4 miles to a four-way stop. Turn right at this intersection to stay on 61, which you should follow approximately 3 miles into downtown Anahuac. At the traffic signal/stop sign at the intersection with South Main Street, turn left (south). After about a mile, watch for the park signs, and turn right into the park, go past the ball fields, and follow signs to the boat ramps. There are a large parking lot, restrooms, and picnic facilities in the park.

Fort Anahuac became a Mexican garrison in 1830, chosen for its strategic location guarding the mouth of the Trinity River. It was the site of the first armed confrontation between Anglo-Texans and Mexican troops on June 10–12, 1832. William B. Travis and other Texans had been imprisoned in the fort; their rescue was the objective of the assault. After their success, the Texans dismantled the fort. Mexican forces attempted to rebuild it in 1835, but Texans

Immature white ibises sunning themselves on a warm winter day

burned the wood for repairs and the fort was never active again.

Fort Anahuac Park, marking the point of the original garrison, is a favorite starting point for trips to the Trinity River's delta area, the area where it deposits its silt load and empties into the Trinity Bay portion of Galveston Bay. This area is very dynamic, ever changing with patterns of rainfall upstream and tropical storms downstream, so that sandbars, large and small, are shifting constantly. Even the most recent maps and aerial photography can be inaccurate. Wind patterns and tidal variations can make a quick change from 12 inches of paddleable water to 2 inches of water on top of oozing mudflats. I have had to claw through the mud to get in or out, the bottom being too soft to stand on and the water being too shallow to float my boat. It's all part of the great adventure of being out and about on Galveston Bay.

Boat ramps here see a steady stream of powerboat launching, so be careful. Using the natural banks is a good way to stay out of their way and make it safer for you to get in and out of your boat.

Bird-watching from walkways in the park and a big Alligator Festival in September are popular activities. As the name of the festival implies, there are plenty of alligators. I have never paddled here on a warm day when I haven't seen several.

■ *Paddling Note.* For my first foray into the area, I chose the Fort Anahuac site. Let me reiterate here the need for a good, recent map and the most recent aerial photograph available. A compass or other reliable navigation aid is a necessity—it is very easy to get turned around in the marshes, and seated in a kayak or canoe, you cannot see over the top of the marsh grasses to get your bearings if indeed there are even good markers to look for.

Mudflats exposed on Trinity Bay at low tide

From the park, my friend Marilyn and I headed south down the Trinity River Channel (rather than the Anahuac Channel, where the present-day Trinity River flows), past mile marker 15, where we entered the channel to green channel marker 9, where we turned right (west) into Trinity Bay. At the water level of that day (5.8 feet on the Trinity River gage at Liberty, 0806700; but remember this area is tidal; tides were peaking at 2 feet at the Eagle Point tide gage, many miles across the bay) we had no trouble getting over the sand flats here; another trip several years later found us walking and dragging our boats across the sand flats, so watch the water levels, the wind direction, and tides if you're going to paddle this route. Because of the exposure to the open bay waters, this trip is recommended only for sea kayaks.

As soon as you enter the bay, you will notice existing and capped oil-drilling activities. We paddled past one of the larger installations close to our path north-northwest to the tip of the Southwest Pass and then northwest to Long Island Bayou. Our intent was to make this a circular trip; from Long Island Bayou to the Old River Cutoff and then down the Trinity River, the Anahuac Channel, Trinity River Channel, and back

to Fort Anahuac. However, as Marilyn and I are wont to do on our trips, we began talking and chasing wildflower photos of swamp lilies so completely missed the concrete wall that clearly marked the turn to the Old River Cutoff channel. However, our travels took us on up into Round Lake, with a turnaround for me in a sea of alligator weed (yes, in the photo my kayak is floating in at least a foot of water).

We reoriented ourselves, lunched under cypress seedlings, and found our way back on course. As the Trinity paralleled the south bank of Lake Anahuac, we started noticing the sound of running water and realized it was overflow from the lake cutting through the trees along the shore and emptying into the river. We waded the concrete spillway for Lake Anahuac and cooled off by soaking in the water before we got back in our boats and paddled on. On this August day, we were surprised to see a large flock of white pelicans on the bay. I had imagined them to be largely winter visitors, but apparently they don't all leave when the warm weather sets in. The length of the trip without wrong turns is about 12 to 15 miles, paddleable in sea kayaks in about 6 hours, including a lunch break.

▲ The author getting a close-up view of a pumping station on Trinity Bay. Photo by Marilyn Kircus

◀ Floating on a bed of alligator weed. Photo by Marilyn Kircus

Adventuring from Anahuac II: The Southwest Pass That Isn't

I intended to share the same paddle trip just described with a friend visiting from Louisiana. The conditions this day were very different. The wind was prevailing from the west but turning to come from the north. Let my experience stand as an example—under these conditions the bay starts emptying its water, and places that floated a boat before no longer do. The same tide gage on the previous trip read levels at 0; the river was 11 feet at Liberty, so you can see the tide is more important in predicting paddleability in shallow-water areas than the mean river flow farther upstream.

We set out again from Fort Anahuac Park. The winds were blowing about 17 miles per hour. We were protected from the wind fairly well while we were in the Trinity River Channel, but the wind was directly in our faces as we headed out into the open bay waters. After several miles of beating into the wind, one of my companions had had enough, so we decided to shorten our trip by cutting across Southwest Pass, which we thought would also protect us somewhat from the wind. Our first attempt at finding the Southwest Pass was unsuccessful; we were too far south and east. We did get to observe close-up the damping effects the seagrasses in this area have on the wind-generated waves, but a little farther on we successfully located the mouth of Southwest Pass and thought we were going to be able to proceed on the altered course. Unfortunately, this is the proof of the "find the latest map and photo" credo for this dynamic landscape. I have located said navigation information since my return and realize that Southwest Pass no longer connects to the Trinity. The older map in my map case that day showed that it did. For our learning experience, we also practiced the fingers-in-the-mud technique of dragging kayaks forward, until the sheer futility of the exercise came home to us. We weren't the only ones being educated that day—many juvenile redfish were in the same condition, and several times I could have grabbed them

with my hands, as they were in water too shallow for them to swim. The soft clay bottoms here were too soft to stand on. I had sunk at least to my knees when I realized the sinking was not going to stop; fortunately, I was able to pull myself out of the mud before the situation became hopeless.

The mudflats offered a feast for many wading birds, including black-necked stilts. As we rounded the bend of one blind lead into a dead-end lake, we encountered a flock of ten or twelve roseate spoonbills that flew off before I could even aim my camera. The more paddleable lakes were ringed by short-blooming sagittaria, and moor hens skittered about. The most unusual insect life was the hundreds of grasshoppers crawling and chewing among the swamp lilies and sagittaria. It was amazing to me they hadn't denuded the place—perhaps their stay here was of short duration. Even in these remote backwaters, stands of water hyacinth were taking root. This is definitely swamp and marsh country and home of many large alligators.

Our thrashing about in the swamps brought us close to a high ridge of ground that supported a fish camp. We could hear motorboats running through a pass that obviously would have been deep enough for us also to float, but we were never able to get to it. We turned around and retraced our route. By the time we neared the Trinity River Channel, the winds died down but the water was clearly gone from the sand flats outside the channel. We ended up pulling our boats for at least some distance over the not-quite-solid bottom. We were on the water only about 5 hours this day.

Another circular trip from Fort Anahuac Park also heads south and west but then navigates for Jacks Pass and via it into the Trinity. Large snags have been known to block its mouth right at the Trinity, so be forewarned that you may have to deal with that before completing a circle. That would make the round-trip 6 to 8 miles.   *July 2004*

Picketts Bayou

Since my misadventure looking for Picketts Bayou, a new access point from Champion Lake to the bayou opened in late 2008. A 2-mile, beautifully wooded open stretch of Picketts Bayou is available from a boat launch only a hundred yards from Champion Lake. Access to the Trinity is through a complicated network of small, twisting tributaries and connections, including a small movable dam that prevents saltwater intrusion. See directions in the following Champion Lake section.

Champion Lake

➡ *Directions.* From I-10, take the exit to FM 565, Old River/Winfree. Travel north 3 miles to FM 1409. Turn right on FM 1409 at the traffic signal, and continue for another 3 miles to CR 417. Turn right on CR 417 for 1.8 miles.

Champion Lake is a shallow-water cypress swamp to the west of the Trinity River. Looking at most maps of the area, you wouldn't expect it to be a lake at all. It includes 800 acres of the Trinity River National Wildlife Refuge, which consists of more than 25,000 acres. This is a bottomland, hardwood-forested swamp whose dominant tree species is the cypress. All paddle trails go through the cypress swamp. Motorboats are restricted to 10 horsepower or less or trawling motors, so you won't have to contend with high-speed motorized craft. The park is open sunrise to sunset year-round. It is open to waterfowl hunting in the fall—check with the park office to make sure of dates.

■ *Paddling Note.* The first thing you should do when planning a visit here is to download and print out the map located at www.fws.gov/southwest/refuges/texas/trinityriver/directions.html. Click on the map link at the bottom of the page. With map in hand, your next wise choice is a compass or GPS in case you get turned around in the swamps. I have been advised that the reflectors are for marking hunting stations, not so much trails, so maybe that's why I could not coordinate them with my GPS. Maybe it was operator error—a very good possibility. In any case, the reflectors are

easy to see. If you get lost, the best way to get out is to pick a direction from the point of a compass and follow it in a straight line—you are sure to bump into dry land along one edge or the other of the swamp and should be able to find your way back to the put-in by following the edge of the paddleable area. The distances make this a good choice for a short paddle of 3 to 4 hours. There is no current here at normal (nonflood) water levels, and it is pretty well protected from the wind.

Water levels in Champion Lake are not as affected by river levels as those in Lake Charlotte. The gage at Champion Lake is not online, but a good approximation is to use the gage for the Trinity River in Liberty at the USGS National Water Information Systems site, "Real-Time Water Data for Texas: Streamflow," and gage number 08067000 (http://waterdata.usgs.gov/tx.nwis/current/?type=flow). If that gage reading is above 27 feet, the Champion Lake access will be closed. Water-control structures at Champion hold water at 6 feet on the Champion Lake gage. At 5 feet on that gage, the north end of the lake is dry. A reading of 12 feet on the Champion Lake gage is roughly equivalent to 27 feet at Liberty. During the drought of 2011, Champion Lake was not paddleable.

During nesting season, generally March through July, you are forbidden to get within 200 yards of an active rookery, and rookeries are fairly extensive on the northern and western parts of the lake. This is also not a good place to paddle early in the morning during waterfowl hunting season!

The US Fish and Wildlife Service has developed a Web site for the refuge and Champion Lake that is a good resource (www.fws.gov/southwest/refuges/texas/trinityriver/).

Turtle Bayou

➡ *Directions.* Take I-10 east from Houston about 30 miles, and exit at TX 61, Hankamer. Go south on 61 a very short distance; just beyond the Exxon station on the right (east) side of the road is the entrance to White Memorial Park. The sign for White Park Church of Christ is the most prominent one at the turn. Turn

"Exploratory" Trip of March 2005

SEVEN intrepid HCC paddlers met at 1:00 p.m. on March 20, 2005, to check out Champion Lake and the boating trails of Trinity River National Wildlife Refuge. The weather was right up there next to perfection: the cypress swamp here and there sporting its spring green look, but most trees still bare.

Six paved parking spots (including a handicapped parking space) are available right at the boat ramp and allow access to the levee and the fishing pier. The park was new at the time, so we were surprised at how many people were there—other than we kayakers, mostly family groups and fishers. The levee has a nice walking trail on it for about a quarter mile. One side is Champion Lake; the other is Picketts Bayou.

From the boat dock, we started south and west along the well-marked trail to three orange reflectors that marked the second trail to the north and marker 9. The bird rookery north and west of trail marker 9 is closed to travel from March 1 until summer. Luckily for us, the unmapped but white-reflector-marked trail that goes from markers 9 to 16 still afforded a circular trip. By yet another unmapped trail, we found marker 8, and then on around the channel to markers 4 and 3. By this point, the channel opens up. Marker 3 sits off on the side on its own private lake; somewhere around marker 2 an obliging alligator stayed perched on a log so we all could admire it.

We easily did our tour in 3 hours—truly a pleasant afternoon's paddle. We could see high-water marks on the trees about 3 feet higher than the level we paddled; in some places the water was only 2 feet deep. Some of these trails must be rather difficult for a modest-sized johnboat, but all are easily navigated in kayaks and canoes. Dry lunch or leg-stretching stops were unavailable until we got to the northern parts of the swamp. We also paddled the length of the levee, so estimated paddle distance is 5 miles including that leg.

The character of Turtle Bayou is a lot like that of the Big Thicket streams of points farther east. Its sandy soils support both hardwoods and pines. White Memorial Park provides a very good access point, with no more public accesses upstream, but Lake Anahuac and Bun's Beach downstream.

White Memorial Park is named for James Taylor White, a cattleman and rancher who settled in the area after 1828. At one time his holdings stretched west to Galveston Bay and south to the Gulf of Mexico. The Turtle Bayou Resolutions were signed near White's home in 1832, foreshadowing the Texas Revolution. The town site for the village of Turtle Bayou was right here at White Park. The area is still known as the Turtle Bayou community. Sawmills operated here at the turn of the century, and if you look closely, you may see a relict mill along the bayou. Several shipwrecks have been located where the old Turtle Bay ferry used to operate. At one time the area had a deeper draft and, of course, Lake Anahuac was not closed off at its southern end.

■ *Paddling Note.* To the right from the ramp is upstream. You will shortly pass under I-10 and can go about a mile farther, depending on water conditions. The course of Turtle Bayou is described as "intermittent" in the upper reaches and 18 miles in length, but I believe you would have to do some serious bushwhacking and boat dragging to get more than a few miles upstream. So turn around and head back to the boat ramp, or go down to Lake Anahuac.

The small tributary to Turtle Bayou entering at the park is Whites Bayou. If the water is high enough, the bayou can be paddled for several miles, as can Albritton Gully to the north of the I-10 corridor.

right into the park, staying to the right past the rodeo arena, going beyond to a parking area and boat ramp. Put your boat in the water at the ramp.

Turtle Bayou originally emptied into Turtle Bay, which fed into Trinity Bay. However, a dam was placed just north of Fort Anahuac and the town of Anahuac in an effort to prevent saltwater intrusion into Turtle Bay; the newly created body of water was renamed Lake Anahuac.

Lake Anahuac

Lake Anahuac is about 2 miles south of White Memorial Park via Turtle Bayou. In 1902 saltwater encroachment in the bay forced the newly formed Trinity River Irrigation District to build a barrier at its southern end to impound freshwater for rice irrigation. The barrier was destroyed by the 1915 hurricane

Dave Kitson paddling the
upper reaches of Champion
Lake

Champion Lake and Picketts Bayou

A canoe, a kayak, and a sailing kayak heading up Turtle Bayou

but rebuilt in 1935. Today the lake is managed by the Chambers-Liberty County Navigation District. There is a nonautomated water-level gage, but if you need to check it, you must call the Navigation District at 409-267-3541. The "usual" level for the lake is 4 feet. However, at lower levels (1.5 feet when I paddled it in mid-winter 1999) there is a beautiful white sandbar exposed on the left as you enter the lake, as well as a stand of cypress trees. If you continue to your right along the lakeshore (you may have to stand well off the shore to find enough water to paddle at a 1.5-foot water level), you will come to Bun's Beach, a beautiful white sand beach and a Chambers County park. The park is open only June–September (the entry gate is locked otherwise), but it is okay to land boats and stretch the legs here at other times of the year. We found it to be a birding hot spot for white ibises in the winter.

Old River

➡️ *Directions.* To get to the put-in, take I-10 east of Houston to Exit 803 (Cove, Old River, Winfree), which is FM 565. Travel north on 565 about 3 miles to the traffic signal at the intersection with FM 1409. Turn right (east) on 1409, and follow it about a half mile to its crossing of the Old River. You will see a historical marker for Old River just before the crossing—*slow down* and pull off onto the easement on your right, just before the crossing. This rutted area is used locally for launching johnboats and other small craft. It is totally unimproved, so I don't suggest using it if it's been raining for a while. It gets deeply rutted, and the ground is quite soft when wet.

You will see a nice wide area for launching on the river. The trip described here heads upriver (to the left, under the bridge and beyond). Heading downriver (to the right; there is so little current that it is sometimes difficult to tell) gives access to Old River Cutoff or to more open waters of Old River Lake and Lost River before rejoining the Trinity River farther downstream.

Old River is an abandoned channel of the current Trinity River and names both the town and the river —and there are four other bodies of water named "Old River" in the state of Texas, including one closer to the San Jacinto River. The (Trinity's) Old River rises 2 miles south of Dayton and has a southerly course for 22 miles to its mouth on the Trinity River. This area was one of the earlier European settlements near Houston. Although the main Trinity River current no longer courses through here, it has enough water in it for year-round paddling. Its mostly tree-lined banks promise shade for summertime paddling. In late fall the cypress trees lining its banks shed the last of their foliage and most of the deciduous trees are bare. There are modern homes and a golf course along one bank, but most of the course is natural. The current

Family paddle on Old River's upper stretches

is sluggish if at all—the day I paddled it, the current seemed to be moving upstream, but that could have been wind effects on foliage and branches floating in the water.

■ *Paddling Note.* As you head upstream, most of the way is a wooded bottomland, with cypress trees lining the banks and pines or oaks behind them with palmettos under the trees. Noticeable at the lower reaches are some open pastures that are testimony to the earlier settlements of ranchers and farmers here as early as 1827. The right bank is pretty much as nature created it with few improvements and only a few stretches of open pastureland or clearings. Pipeline crossings are not very intrusive. Like all our local water-ways, this one meanders to all points of the compass but generally trends northwest to the limits of our canoe navigation, perhaps 3 miles upstream from the put-in. Trees across the waterway may limit upstream navigation. At this turnaround, trees touch overhead and a large part of the way has tall timber, giving this good potential for a shaded summer trip as well as a delightful midwinter trip.

Interesting natural features include many vining plants, at least in the upper reaches. As the day became more overcast and late afternoon moved toward dark, a pair of barred owls began calling. One was within 30 feet of the river, up in a tree, and we got close enough to see it wink at us before it retreated farther into the forest. Kingfishers flitted from bank to bank, and robins and cardinals were numerous.

With an 11:00 a.m. put-in time, we arrived back to the same point to load and depart by 4:00 p.m. We took one break and a lunch stop to make this a very easy 5-hour out-and-back trip.

Access to the southernmost reaches of Old River is from the muddy banks of the I-10 bridge at Old River Lake on the western banks or 2 miles farther south from Hugo Point Park.

Old River Lake

Hugo Point Park was opened in 2003 and has direct access to Old River Lake, with multiple boat ramps, covered picnic facility, restrooms, and a large parking lot. There are a multitude of interconnections with other bodies of water in the area: to the Lake Charlotte complex, Old and Lost Rivers, Cotton Lake, Trinity Bay, and the Trinity River Cutoff.

From the same launching place as described for Old River (the FM 1409 river crossing), paddle downstream, or to your right from the access point, until a sizable stream enters this body of water from the left. Turn left on that body of water, and you now find yourself on the Old River Cutoff. The Cutoff is another meander channel from the ever-wandering Trinity River, which is rather narrow but with fairly vertical banks and a flow that again assures year-round paddling access.

In the summer, tall trees on both sides provide welcome shade and good protection from the prevailing southerly breezes from the Gulf. Occasional sandbanks occur and make a good stopping place for you and a small number of friends. Finding an easy place to exit boats can be fairly challenging. Many older sandbars are covered by mature vegetation; frequent flooding in the region (on at least a geologic time scale) rearranges and moves sandbars and watercourses.

■ *Paddling Note.* Not far from where you enter the Cutoff from the Old River Channel, the stream goes around a very large horseshoe curve. A GPS-equipped companion noticed that after we had paddled almost an hour, we had arrived at a spot only 300 yards from where we had started into the horseshoe. That might be the extent of a midsummer paddle. When you look at a map of the area, notice a second horseshoe curve not far from the first one—one can paddle a large number of river miles to get only a short distance by land.

On another trip, two companions and I searched in vain for a connection from the Cutoff to the Trinity River. Beware outdated topo maps—such a connection, if it occurs at all, cannot be found from following any of the maps I was using. Note also that aerial photography (which I discovered after the trip) shows no such connection. We were truly lost on the Lost

Ron Nunnally showing off his newly built canoe at the Old River/Cutoff put-in

Paddling the Cutoff

and never did find it. It is a very pretty marsh/swamp paddle, however.

John Wiggins Bayou

The access to John Wiggins Bayou is about a 4-mile paddle from the put-in described for Lost River and Lost Lake, under I-10 close to the FM 565 exit (see also the following map for the Lake Charlotte Complex). The long paddle is well worth it, up and across Lost River. The "ferry" marked on older maps has long since been out of business and lies rusting by the side of the river. A bridge spans the river now. Just beyond it, go right and your are in John Wiggins Bayou, pristine and untouched (see map of Lake Charlotte Complex). During the winter season it is loaded with waterfowl. Its remote access, far from motorboat launches, seems to make it a haven for the birds. On a midwinter day hundreds of pintail ducks flushed with a thunderous beating of wings that sounded like a jet engine at takeoff. Hundreds of white ibises and snow geese were there, too. The paddle route goes through pastureland, by an oil field (and attendant bridge), and through magnificent swampland. Four miles of access paddle are followed by only a few miles of bayou, but it is lovely to see.

Lake Charlotte Complex

Four lakes, Charlotte, Mac, Mud, and Miller, are the major features of this complex. Their interconnections, including the passes, bayous, and twisting stream, make many interesting trips possible. Lake Pass also offers direct access to Lake Charlotte.

Lake Charlotte
➜ *Directions.* The easiest and most direct access to Lake Charlotte is from Cedar Hill Park on its northeast corner. To get there, travel I-10 about 30 miles east of Houston and take Exit 810 (Anahuac, Liberty, FM 563). Follow FM 563 north about 2.8 miles. Turn left (west) on Lake Charlotte Road, which is well marked. In another 1.1 miles, the entrance to the park is on your left. There is no sign marking the entrance,

River. Beware swamp trips in this active region! We paddled over 20 miles that day and in circles at least three times to the same spot before giving up and paddling home the same way we had come many hours earlier. Whether you want to paddle a short distance or a long one, this is a pretty, shaded spot to get out in the woods.

Lost River and Lost Lake

This part of the Old/Lost/Trinity complex seems particularly well named. The access to Lost River, Lost Lake, and John Wiggins Bayou is a "creative" one on the north side of I-10, on the west side of Old River Lake, and is not improved in any way. It is accessed only from the westbound lanes of I-10 at Exit 803 (Cove, Old River, Winfree). If you come to the intersection with 565, you are too far west. Where we put boats in the water is literally under the I-10 elevated highway. The map in this book makes the connection between Lost River and Trinity look easier and more straightforward than it is. I spent the better part of a day looking for it

Sunset on Lost River Lake.
Photo by Marilyn Kircus

but a good landmark is the Sherman Cemetery, which is directly across from the park entrance. If you pass it, you will have to make a sharp right-hand turn and then turn around. Drive down the park entrance road until you can see the water. This park has nice picnic facilities, pit toilets, and plenty of parking for a day on the water.

Lake Charlotte is the largest of a complex of at least four lakes that lie to the east of the Trinity River in Chambers County, just north of I-10. Although it is only 30 miles from downtown Houston, the largest westernmost cypress swamp in Texas seems a universe away. The area teems with wildlife. Summer visitors can be rewarded with the sight of hundreds of shorebirds feeding on the shallow lake bottom. Winter avian visitors include many migratory species. Beavers and alligators live along Lake Pass. Paddlers on a recent Houston Canoe Club trip saw a herd of

Mac Lake

Trinity River

Mac Bayou

Lost River

Willow Cove

Cedar Hill Park

Lake Charlotte Rd

Lake Charlotte

Buzzard Roost

West Cove

John Wiggins Bayou

Bird Island

Sand Pt

Mud Lake

Mud Lake Bayou

Lake Miller

Lake Pass

Lake Charlotte Complex

I 10

0 .5 1

W N E S

wild hogs. White ibises, night herons, and many other birds nest in the area. Large wasp nests are found here, too, some at head or paddle height, so keep your eyes open! Snakes of many varieties sun themselves on shrubs or hang out on branches to watch for prey below.

Once you are back in the swamps and lakes of this area, it is easy to get turned around and lose your bearings. A good map and a compass and/or a GPS are highly recommended. The entrance to the Mud Lake pass from Lake Charlotte in particular is difficult to locate. Our GPS reading put the entryway in the middle of Lake Charlotte, not even at its shoreline, so beware and watch very carefully where you have been going so you can find your return path.

If you have a GPS, be sure to take a reading at Cedar Hill Park. Notice the material you are standing on as you launch your boats: these are the shells of rangia clams, and you are standing on an ancient Native American midden dating back several hundred years. These clams lived in the muddy bottoms of the lakes. They would be considered to be off-flavor by modern standards, but they were an important food for the original inhabitants, who consumed them in large numbers and left piles of discarded shells throughout the area. Changes in the composition of the lake waters greatly decreased their numbers, and few if any are to be found today. If you look up, you will see several native pecan trees, an added source of food for those who lived here, probably Attacapa or Orcoquisac peoples.

Mac Bayou and Mac Lake

Heading west from Cedar Hill Park, you will come to the entrance to Mac Bayou. Ten years ago this bayou was dammed, so a portage was required to continue down it. Major flooding removed that obstruction and brought lots of silt into Lake Charlotte. The access to the bayou from the lake is now marked by bright green willow saplings on the sand island during the warm months of the year. When you head out the bayou toward Mac Lake, you need to travel diagonally across an intersecting wide cut to continue to Mac

Linda Day and her dog Chipper emerging from the willow thicket hanging over Lake Pass entrance

Lake. The wide cut is human-made and leads to a dock, now in disrepair and almost unnoticeable upstream (to the right). The dock area is some of the highest ground around and a good spot for a lunch or rest stop, but no facilities or running water is available.

Mac Lake, at the upper end of Mac Bayou, is a long finger of a lake ringed by cypress trees. Mac Bayou and the intersecting cut can be paddled at any water level adequate to get there from Cedar Hill

Park, but the lake can become too shallow to navigate any distance at water levels below 7.0 on the gage for Lake Charlotte. The online gage can be found at http://waterdata.usgs.gov/tx/nwis/uv/?site_no=08067118&PARAmeter_cd=00065,00060. You should be aware that this gage does not function below the reading of 6.8; for example, if the actual water level is the equivalent of 4.5, the gage still shows 6.8. If you make a left (southwest) turn in the cut, you will travel downstream to join the Trinity River.

If, instead of going west from Cedar Hill Park, you head due south, you will notice (if you look closely!) another shell-covered landing spot. This is also a good place for a rest stop or lunch break. There are not many high and consistently dry spots around where

◄◄◄ *Paul Woodcock and Mary Zaborowski enjoying Mac Lake in summer*

◄◄ *Cypress trees bare of foliage in midwinter on Mac Bayou*

◄ *Duckweed covering Mac Bayou passage*

you can get out of a boat. Slightly to the west of the landing spot and along the shoreline is the entrance to Mud Lake. Its GPS coordinates are UTM 15R0333483 3304520; longitude N 29°51'36", latitude W 94°43'26.2". The passage is barely the width of a canoe at some places and difficult to locate—in high water I paddle the south shore of Lake Charlotte, look for an open space in the trees that indicates a body of water, and paddle directly through the trees, but that technique doesn't work well at lower levels.

Mud Lake

Despite its name, Mud Lake is the prettiest of the cypress-lined lakes in this region. At its northeastern corner is an important bird rookery, which is closed to paddlers during nesting season. Night herons, white ibises, and many other birds nest there. Bald eagles are occasionally seen in the area. My favorite paddling passageway is the route between Mud and Miller lakes. It must be a relict of an older Trinity River Channel, when more water would have flowed between the lakes—it is quite deep (by the standards of this area) for most of its length. At points it is 20 to 30 feet wide. Duckweed grows here in profusion when the weather is warm enough. The water is occasionally crystal clear, so you can see the garfish swimming beneath you—and on occasion a baby alligator. When the buttonbushes are blooming, butterflies are everywhere. Cypress trees surround the lake, but there are deciduous hardwoods as well and thickets of water shrubs. Its southern terminus at Lake Miller is typically choked with alder, so expect to have to push through the shrubs as you near the lakeshore.

Miller Lake

Miller Lake is the southernmost of the Lake Charlotte Complex, and the one from which the traffic noise of I-10 is the most noticeable. At one time it had more direct access to the Trinity River and in the late eighteenth century was the site of Joseph Blancpain's trading post. War of 1812 veteran Henry Miller had his homesite here, under the large oak trees on the south shoreline. Houston Canoe Club placed a geocache near his memorial plaque. Wild grapes grow here in profusion, and cypress knees guard the shoreline. To my chagrin, I also found the one steel rebar hiding among the knees and poked a hole in my canoe, so

be careful! I know from that incident that uphill on the south side is a walkable trail that will eventually bring you to the frontage road for I-10, a very usable escape route if your canoe is sinking. Miller Lake is reachable either by the passage from Mud Lake or from a side channel of Lake Pass.

Lake Pass

Lake Pass for many years was the access point of choice for canoe trips to the Lake Charlotte area. It connects the southwestern corner of Lake Charlotte with the Trinity River, a paddling distance of approximately 2 miles. Its entrance to Miller Lake is at Miller Lake's northwestern corner. There are several overhanging shrubs where the pass goes into Miller Lake—rarely have I been there on a warm day that at least one snake has not jumped out of those shrubs and

Pickerelweed in full bloom along the "Sulphur Cut" at Mac Bayou

into the water on my approach. Paddling up Lake Pass even in the heat of a summer evening is quite pleasant, or at least as pleasant as it gets when the air temperature and the humidity are in the 90s. The pass is shaded by cypress trees and is deep enough that it can be paddled year-round. In the winter, the trees provide a nice windbreak. The pass is periodically choked by black willows that have fallen into the water.

Cotton Lake

➡️ *Directions.* From Houston, take I-10 east to Exit 803 (Cove, Old River, Winfree). Drive south on FM 565 for approximately 0.8 mile to the intersection with FM 3246/Gou Hole Road. Turn left on Gou Hole Road, and follow it approximately 0.7 mile to Maley Road. Go right on Maley Road, and drive slowly through this residential area. The next intersection has a sign with a left arrow pointing to the "Boat Ramp" at Hugo Point Park, which is not the direct access for Cotton Lake. Turn right at the intersection for the Cotton Lake ramp.

Cotton Lake is due east of Houston, about 35 miles from downtown. This is a true coastal wetland area, a spawning ground and nursery for many forms of aquatic and wetland life. It's a good place to see wading birds, from herons to roseate spoonbills, and occasional alligators. In the spring, swamp lilies and Louisiana iris are blooming in profusion. Wild hibiscus blooms in summer. There are few tall trees, so expect a lot of sun exposure. In fall and winter there are a lot of ducks and geese and plenty of hunters. Alligators are common.

This trip requires at least 3 hours and can take all day. You can do an out-and-back trip, paddle through the bayous and inlets to Trinity Bay, or paddle down one bayou and back another. A good map and navigation skills are imperative here and for many other bodies of water in this area. If your trip takes you to a cement levee, do not cross it. On the other side is the cooling pond for a power-generating station, where you are not welcome in this water or even lunching on the levee.

■ *Paddling Note.* From the public boat launch a line of sticks marks the boat channel southeast over to Horse Bayou. Hurricane Ike deposited a thick layer of silt at this put-in. At low water levels, it is no longer usable. Look over your shoulder on the way out to see what to look for on the return trip. Shortly, the bayou branches. The left branch goes to Old River Lake. If you stay to the right, you take Horse Bayou into the marsh. Look for channels that lead south to Trinity Bay.

Sometimes the water is high enough to paddle all the way down the easternmost channel. You can paddle west just before a few houses on the levee road, which is on the south and east sides of the marsh. Sometimes the water runs out before you get that far, and you will have to find alternative channels running east. A portage is possible, but the mosquitoes get very hungry for human flesh when you disturb them by stirring up the grasses and bushes. You can also stay farther north and take main channels down to Trinity Bay, where there is usually a tiny beach to have your lunch

To get back, work your way to the west and north to Red Bayou/High Tree Bayou, which can be paddled back into Cotton Lake at its southwest end. There is a large rock levee along the south shore that is the boundary of the cooling lake. Power plant personnel do not want paddlers on those rocks. So, if you want to take out for a rest, stay close to the water. Take one of the openings back into the lake proper, and set a course approximately northeast to get back to the take-out.

Trinity Bay West

The west side of Trinity Bay, despite having a road running along it, has only one public access point to the water, at McCollum Park. It's a nice little park but has a high, steep bank down to the water—it wouldn't be hard to get a boat down to the water, but it's not going to be fun on the return trip. Trinity Bay North and Trinity Bay West are best accessed from Fort Anahuac Park.

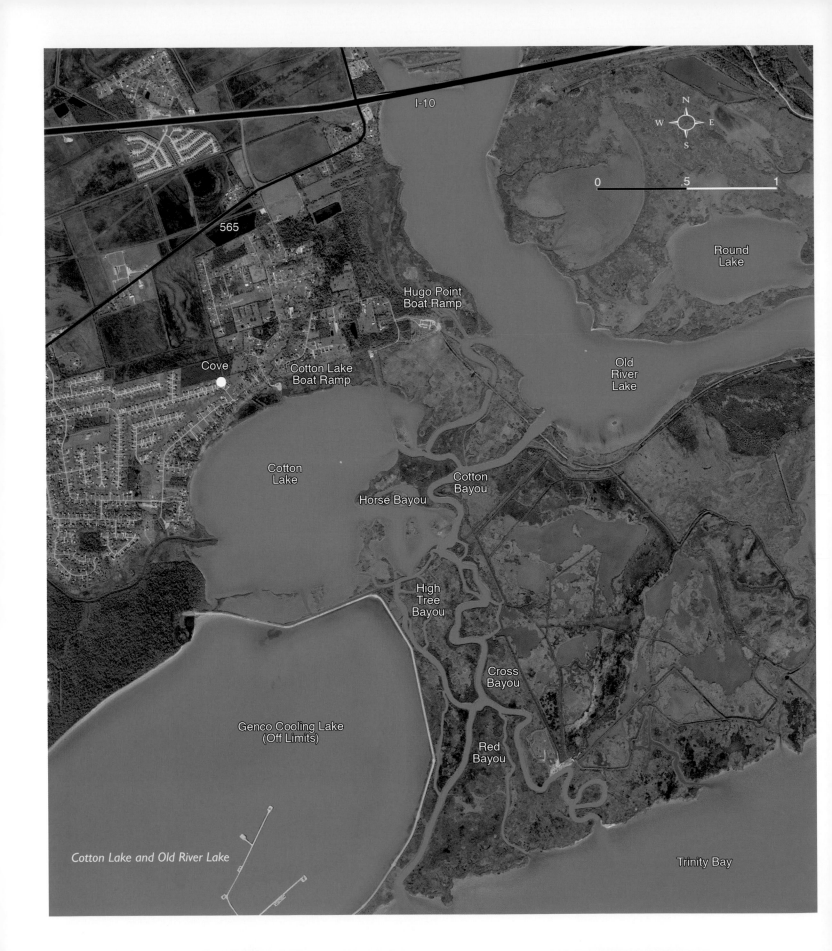

Cotton Lake and Old River Lake

Houston Association of Sea Kayakers paddling down Cross Bayou from Cotton Lake. Photo by Marilyn Kircus

Mixed craft of Houston Canoe Club Members at shell midden lunch stop on west shore of Trinity Bay

The warty bark of the "toothache tree," or prickly ash, atop a Trinity Bay midden

Facilities

Trinity River System

Paddling area	Access point	Toilet	Picnic	Camping	Water	Ramp	Parking	Gage	Mileage	Comments
Above Lake Livingston:								08065800	5	
Bedias Creek										
Lake Livingston									30	
Double Lake Recreation Area				●						
Trinity River Access Points										
	Access 1: Below Lake Livingston dam	●	●		●	●	●		11	Fee
	Access 2: US 59 crossing					●	●	08066250	14	
	Access 3: Menard Creek							08066300	8	
	Access 4: FM 787 crossing							08066500	30	
	Access 5: TX 105 crossing								30	
	Access 6: US 90 crossing							08067000	24	
	Access 7: Port Street boat ramp	●				●	●		2	TPWD ramp
	Access 8: Moss Bluff/ Picketts Bayou stretch								12	
	Access 9: I-10 crossing								2	
	Access 10: Mayes Trace/ Trinity River Island Recreation Area	●				●	●		2	Visitors Center
	Access 11: Port of Anahuac								1	
	Access 12: Fort Anahuac Park	●	●		●	●	●			

Facilities: Trinity River System

Paddling area	Access point	Toilet	Picnic	Camping	Water	Ramp	Parking	Gage	Mileage	Comments
Picketts Bayou							●			
	Picketts Bayou boat ramp	●				●	●		3	
Champion Lake										
	Champion Lake boat ramp	●					●	●	3	Gage not automated
Turtle Bayou										
	White Memorial Park	●	●			●	●			
Lake Anahuac									10	
Old River									4	
Old River Lake						●	●		12	
	Hugo Point Park	●	●			●	●			
	Old River Cutoff								22	
	FM 1409 crossing									
Lost River and Lost Lake									9	
	I-10 crossing									
John Wiggins Bayou									4	
Lake Charlotte Complex										
	Lake Charlotte	●	●				●	08067118	1	Access from Cedar Hill Park
	Mac Bayou and Mac Lake								2	Access from Cedar Hill Park
	Mud Lake								0.25	Access from Cedar Hill Park
	Miller Lake								0.5	Access from Cedar Hill Park
	Lake Pass								2	Access from I-10
Cotton Lake						●	●		5	
Trinity Bay West									5	Access to Trinity Bay West and Trinity Bay North from Fort Anahuac Park

3 Trinity–San Jacinto Basin

BETWEEN THE TRINITY RIVER BASIN and the San Jacinto Basin is a relatively small area drained by Cedar Bayou and Goose Creek. All directions to access points begin in Baytown.

Cedar Bayou

This bayou is surpassed only by Buffalo Bayou and the Houston Ship Channel for number and size of refineries and chemical plants along its shores. Scouting the area north of I-10 for possible put-ins, I found myself right in the middle of the Mont Belvieu megaplex, and there are several others before the water mixes with Galveston Bay. The upper stretches appear too narrow and overgrown with trees and shrubs to be a comfortable paddle. I recommend you put in farther downstream on the bayou, from a tributary called Cary Bayou, at Holloway Park. Another site to check out is from the eastbound frontage road along I-10. The upper stretches in particular look much like East Texas streams with white sand beaches and stands of large pine trees, giving way to the flat and open coastal marshes at the mouth of the bayou on Tabbs Bay.

Access 1: Holloway Park

➡ *Directions.* Holloway Park is located at 4219 Raccoon Drive. From TX 146, turn west on Massey Tomkins Drive (just south of where 146 crosses Cedar Bayou), then right (north) on Raccoon Drive. The first turn to your left takes you into the park to the put-in for Cary Bayou.

Cary Bayou is just big enough to float your boat and within a quarter mile empties into Cedar Bayou. It is 5.5 miles from here to Roseland Park. Holloway Park has tennis courts, an outdoor basketball court, and a children's playground, but no restroom facilities. New homes surround the park, truly a suburban setting.

An alternative paddle is to go upstream on Cedar Bayou. The banks are mostly forested, with the occasional home along the water. You can expect a lot of pine trees and forest most of the length. I have paddled 5 miles upstream from Holloway Park and found it delightful. My experiences have been during the cooler days of winter. Expect a lot more motorboat traffic during the summer and on warm days.

Access 2: Roseland Park

Roseland Park, located at 100 Roseland Drive, is a very large park with pavilions and plenty of covered picnic tables, even down at the waterfront. A large boat ramp and equally large paved parking lot are at the far end of the park. As you face the ramps from the parking lot, on your left is a side channel with concrete riprap sides that is sometimes an easier place to put a canoe or kayak in the water than dropping it off the bulkheaded banks, but take your choice. Full restroom facilities are available here. This is a very popular place for water skiers and Jet Skis, so expect to see a lot of them on the water.

Access 3: Thompson's Fish Camp

Thompson's Fish Camp is on the bay to the west at Cedar Bayou's mouth, accessed on land from Tri City Beach Road. On the bayou itself is Crawley's Seafood ramp. Both are commercial, for-fee establishments, and both took a direct hit and high-water surge from Hurricane Ike. What makes access to either one of them "interesting" is that the FM 2354 (Tri City Beach Road) bridge no longer exists, so you can't change

0 1 2

Highlands
Reservoir

San Jacinto
River

Cedar
Bayou

10

565

146

330

Goose
Creek

Cary
Bayou

Burnet
Bay

Holloway
Park

Scott
Bay

Baytown

1405

Point Barrow

Roseland
Park

Fred Hartman
Bridge

146

55

2354

Tabbs
Bay

Thompsons
Fish Camp

Beach
City

Trinity
Bay

Atkinson Island

Houston Point

Trinity–San Jacinto Basin

Goose Creek and Cedar Bayou

Holloway Park on Cedar Bayou

your mind en route without having to do a lot of backtracking to make up for it. Because these are off the natural channel of Cedar Bayou, make sure you don't take the barge channel instead or you will miss your take-out and/or have a longer paddle to get there!

Atkinson Island

The Port of Houston has developed canoe trails on Atkinson Island that can be accessed from Thompson's Fish Camp. Getting to Atkinson Island's Demonstration Marsh trails involves crossing open bay waters, which adds a considerable element of danger and exposure. Sea kayaks are the recommended craft.

The marsh demonstrates the beneficial use of dredged material to create an intertidal marsh and fishery habitat and to improve the water quality of Galveston Bay. The paddling trails begin at the beach.

Goose Creek

The City of Baytown has converted a lot of the waterfront along Goose Creek, particularly in its lower reaches, to parkland, making this a very recreation-friendly place to float, stroll, bike, have a picnic, or simply sit by the banks and watch the world go by.

People in the petroleum industry may equate Goose Creek to the oil fields that take their name from the body of water. This is the site of some of the earliest oil wells in Texas, including some of the first offshore

Beautifully wooded banks of Cedar Bayou between Holloway Park and Roseland Park

drilling, and you can see plenty of the remnants of that today. Humble Oil, which later became Exxon, built its first refinery in Baytown. Today this is an enormous operation just off TX 146.

The entire stretch of water described for Goose Creek is 4 miles total, so you could start from any point, paddle upstream and downstream and back to your starting point, and have an easy paddle. Wind will be a factor. In July 2006 I put in at the Wetlands Center with several friends, paddled far upstream past Rollingbrook Drive, and was eventually stopped by a pipe crossing the stream above water level. Flooding several weeks earlier had draped many of the trees with plastic bags and miscellaneous "civilized" trash items, but otherwise the creek was quite natural and a

nice paddle. We saw white pelicans and many kinds of wading birds, and the most swamp lilies I've seen in our area. Many were in bloom, and it is likely you will be able to enjoy some plants' blooms almost any month of the year. They line the banks of Goose Creek.

The observation dock in the photograph is sitting atop a mudflat exposed by northerly winds and low tide on a late December day. Under most other conditions you can paddle right up to the dock. A second photo of the same dock, taken in June, shows what it looks like in the summer and at higher tides. Subsidence has been a real problem in this area; before the 1970s it is likely Goose Creek did not spread out like this. The land has dropped 5 to 10 feet, making more of the area prone to flooding.

Access 1: Walker Park

This nice little park, located off Garth Road at 704 Riverbend Street, gives grassy-bank access to the east fork of Goose Creek. Be sure to scout under the Garth Road bridge before you take your boats down to the stream; at moderate water levels you can float under the bridge fairly easily; at low water you may have to lift your boat over a pipe; at high water, don't put in, or you will scrape your head on the bridge and the water will obviously be too high for safe paddling. It is about a mile and half upstream of Decker Nature Center.

Access 2: Decker Nature Center, Goose Creek Trail

Decker Nature Area is located on Decker Drive, just south of TX 146. There is a good parking area here and a view of the water, but access is unimproved. Hiking is available on Goose Creek Trail. You will need to carry your boats and equipment about

▲ *Mudflats exposed on Goose Creek at low tide in winter*

◄ *A much higher tide on Goose Creek in summer, bringing enough water to float a boat*

Swamp lilies growing along the banks of Goose Creek

100 feet to the bank and the small T-dock that fishers often use. It may be easier to simply head downstream about half a mile to Goose Creek Park to put in.

Access 3: Goose Creek Park

Goose Creek Park is located at 3 Price Street. Look for the sign on Texas Avenue just east of its crossing with Goose Creek. There is a huge covered picnic pavilion and several smaller ones right next to the water. Permanent restroom facilities are available, and it is a short carry from the parking lot to the grassy banks of the stream. As you face the small pavilion in the water (the one in the photos), on its left side is a ramp that should make it quite easy to put your boat in the water. If the water is too low, try again a quarter of a mile downstream at the Eddie V. Gray Wetlands Center.

Access 4: Eddie V. Gray Wetlands Center

The Wetlands Center, located at 1724 Market Street, has a paved parking area and boat ramp. Be sure to visit the Wetlands Center itself if it is open when you are here. Call 281-420-7128 to confirm hours of operation. From the Wetlands Center downstream to Britton Park is 1.7 miles.

Access 5: W. C. Britton Park

W. C. Britton Park, located at 1305 Arizona Street, has lovely park benches and walking trails. Merv's Overlook has a nice overview of the water. From here it is a half mile downstream to McBride boat ramp.

Access 6: V. H. "Buddy" McBride Boat Ramp

This very busy boat ramp, just off the Business 146 crossing of Goose Lake, includes a large paved parking lot but no amenities. I have used this launch also for night paddling along the Houston Ship Channel, pre-9/11—probably not a good idea today as it is a security-sensitive area and you are quite close to the Port of Houston.

From the parking lot you have a great view of the George Hartman Bridge, which carries TX 146 some 178 feet above the Houston Ship Channel. If your route to this site does not involve crossing the bridge, you ought to do it anyway; day or night it's an almost surreal experience. It is like driving through a gigantic three-dimensional sculpture with yellow support cables gleaming in sunlight or artificial illumination to the top of its 400-foot towers.

Highlands Reservoir

Just in case you see this on a map and are tempted to check it out, by all means go and have a look. Bring your fishing rod and tackle, and you can fully enjoy the reservoir—but don't bring your canoe or kayak. Boats are not allowed on the water. It is owned by the San Jacinto River Authority and is a source of drinking water for the City of Houston.

Facilities

Trinity–San Jacinto Basin

Paddling Area	Access point	Toilet	Picnic	Camping	Water	Ramp	Parking	Gage	Mileage	Comments
Cedar Bayou										
	Access 1: Holloway Park		●				●	08067500	5	Playground
	Access 2: Roseland Park	●	●		●	●	●		10	Very large park
	Access 3: Thompson's Fish Camp	●				●	●		4	Fee
	Atkinson Island									
Goose Creek										
	Access 1: Walker Park		●				●		1.5	
	Access 2: Decker Nature Center, Goose Creek Trail						●		0.5	Hiking trail
	Access 3: Goose Creek Park		●				●		0.5	
	Access 4: Eddie V. Gray Wetlands Center		●			●	●	08067525	1	
	Access 5: W. C. Britton Park		●						0.5	
	Access 6: V. H. "Buddy" McBride boat ramp					●	●		0.5	

4 San Jacinto River Basin

"SAN JACINTO" is an important name in Texas history. On the battlefield next to this river Texas won its independence from Mexico on April 21, 1836. As early as 1690 its strategic importance to the Spaniards in Mexico resulted in the construction of the Atascocita Road, which facilitated the movement of troops to defend the area from the French, who were moving west from the Louisiana Territory. The Atascocita Road followed the same path as present-day FM 1960 to the north of Houston. By 1824 American immigrants were settling the area, which was incorporated as part of the Austin Colony. The San Jacinto River formed its easternmost boundary.

The San Jacinto River flows south from Lake Houston, 28 miles to Galveston Bay. The river is incorporated with Buffalo Bayou to form a segment of the Houston Ship Channel. Lake Houston is formed by a dam that backs up over the confluence of the East and West forks of the San Jacinto. Both forks are paddleable and scenic for most of their length. Important tributaries whose canoe trails I will describe, in addition to Buffalo Bayou, are Peach Creek, Luce Bayou, Cypress Creek, and Spring Creek. Farther upstream, the West Fork is dammed to create Lake Conroe. Just to its north is Lake Stubblefield, a popular paddling area.

The San Jacinto River Authority, in combination with the City of Houston, controls the outflow from Lake Conroe. For the latest information on releases and river levels, visit their Web site at www.sjra.net and check the USGS gages.

Lake Conroe

Access 1: Stubblefield Recreation Area

➡ *Directions.* From I-45 north of Conroe, take the exit to FM 1375 near the town of New Waverly and head west. In about 8 miles you will cross Lake Conroe. Two miles past the lake a green road sign and brown recreation sign show the right turn on FSR 215 to Stubblefield Recreation Area. Follow the signage, and in 4 miles you will be at the Stubblefield camp. Ahead of you is the bridge over the West Branch of the San Jacinto River. Cross the bridge to the far side, park, and put your boat on the water.

This is the farthest northern and western part of the San Jacinto watershed described. It falls entirely within the Sam Houston National Forest, has a camping area with twenty-eight sites, and is basically an out-and-back paddle, or with a shuttle you can connect to other public access areas on Lake Conroe.

■ *Paddling Note.* You can head upstream (north) for several miles until the stream becomes too choked to paddle anymore or head downstream (south) onto Lake Conroe. You are traveling the West Fork of the San Jacinto; Lake Conroe begins where the water is backed up. The river is forested its entire length. Unless the killers-of-water-hyacinth or a heavy frost has been at work, you may find yourself, particularly in the lower reaches, blocked by huge drifts of this nasty, but beautiful-flowering, alien invader.

Access 2: Scotts Ridge Recreation Area

➡ *Directions.* From I-45 north of Conroe, exit at FM 1097 and head west. Approximately 1.5 miles past the bridge over Lake Conroe, turn right at the boat ramp sign. Restrooms are available.

This boat ramp is operated by the National Forest Service. A day-use fee is required. Located on the western shores of Lake Conroe, it is a good starting or ending point for a 9- or 10-mile paddle to Stubblefield or any other site of your choosing.

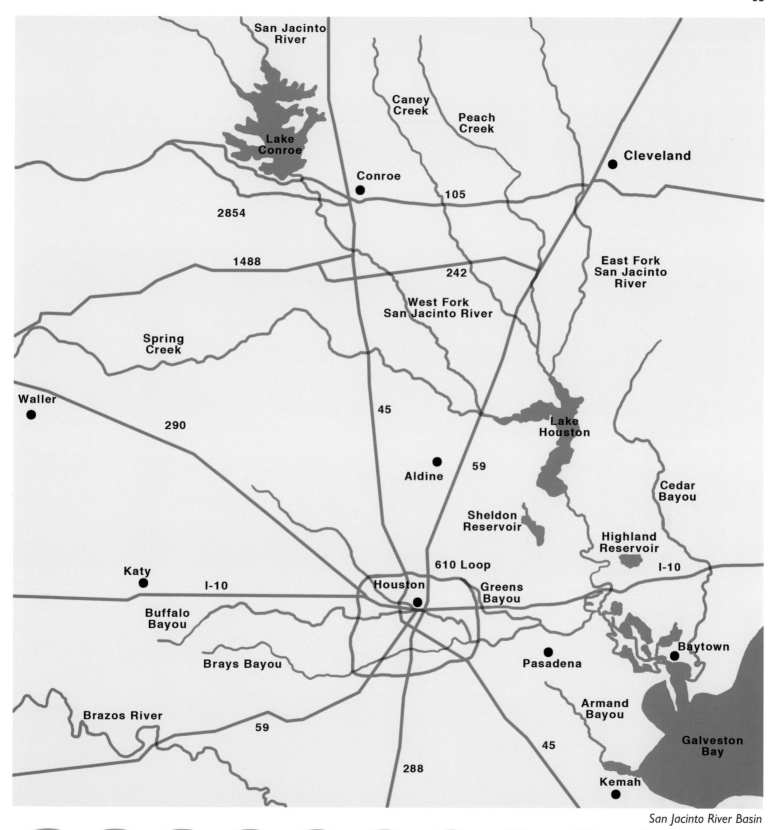

San Jacinto River Basin

San Jacinto River

FSR 216

Stubblefield
Recreation Area

FSR 215

1375

To 45 and New Waverly

149

County
Line Rd

Lake
Conroe

Scotts Ridge
Boat Ramp

45

1097

Boat
Ramp

830

105

Lake Conroe

Upper limits of navigation on West Fork of the San Jacinto River

Access 3: FM 830 Ramp

➡ *Directions.* From I-45 north of Conroe, exit at FM 830. Follow 830 to its end, 5 miles to the west at Lake Conroe. This public, no-fee-required, boat ramp is located on the eastern shores of Lake Conroe.

The boat ramps at both Scotts Ridge and FM 830 will have a considerable amount of motorboat traffic, as will the lake's waters near them. Expect wakes from the watercraft, as well as potential wind effects on the large open lake body. My preferred craft here is the sea kayak. Of course, canoes work, too, but are more affected by both wind and waves.

There are several more commercially operated marinas and for-fee boat ramps that are not discussed here or shown on the map.

Lake Raven

➡ *Directions.* To get to Huntsville State Park, from I-45 just south of Huntsville, take Exit 109. Follow Park Road 40 south and west to the park, about 2 miles.

Two-hundred-acre Lake Raven was formed by damming Big Chinquapin and Little Chinquapin creeks where they merged and flowed on to join Prairie Branch of the San Jacinto. The dam and Huntsville State Park's facilities were originally constructed by the

▲ Kayaks at the ready—
Houston Association of Sea
Kayaks boats at Scotts Ridge
launching place. Photo by
Marilyn Kircus

▶ Palmetto underbrush
against bare trees in winter,
West Fork of the San Jacinto
River

Where the white pelicans are in winter—north shores of Lake Houston. Photo by Marilyn Kircus

Civilian Conservation Corps in the late 1930s. Overnight camping and cabins are available; call 936-295-5644 for more information.

For several years the Houston Canoe Club held its Canoe Rendezvous here, bringing in vendors from across the United States and excellent canoe and kayaking instruction. There is a public swim area on the lake and quiet paddling with several access points, including a few directly from some campsites. There is a canoe livery on-site, so you don't even have to bring your own boat to paddle here.

West Fork, San Jacinto River

This stretch of the San Jacinto, from below Lake Conroe to US 59 at Lake Houston, is heavily forested with tall timber and few signs of civilization. Its flow is determined by releases from Lake Conroe, which was heavily damaged by Hurricane Rita in August 2005. To check on current and projected water releases, visit the San Jacinto River Authority Web site (www.sjra .net). The distance from the TX 105 crossing to the FM 2854 crossing is 4 miles; I-45 is 8 miles farther.

FM 242 is about 5 miles from the I-45 crossing; and from there it is approximately 15 to 18 miles to the US 59 crossing, just downstream of where Spring Creek enters the river. The total distance from TX 105 to US 59 is 34 miles—great potential for a two- or three-day primitive camping trip. Much of this appears to be private property, but unimproved. Downed trees may be a problem on this narrow stream. The water is nice and clear, with a sandy bottom.

Access 1: Edgewater Park

Just beyond the US 59 crossing on the north bank is Edgewater Park. It is a convenient take-out not only for trips on the West Fork of the San Jacinto but also for trips originating at Mercer Arboretum or Jesse Jones Park on Spring Creek and other put-ins for Cypress Creek. There is public parking and access to the river under the 59 bridge, but it is a long walk to the water.

Access 2: River Grove Park

➡ *Directions.* From US 59 northbound, exit just after crossing the West Fork of the San Jacinto River. When you can make a right turn from the frontage

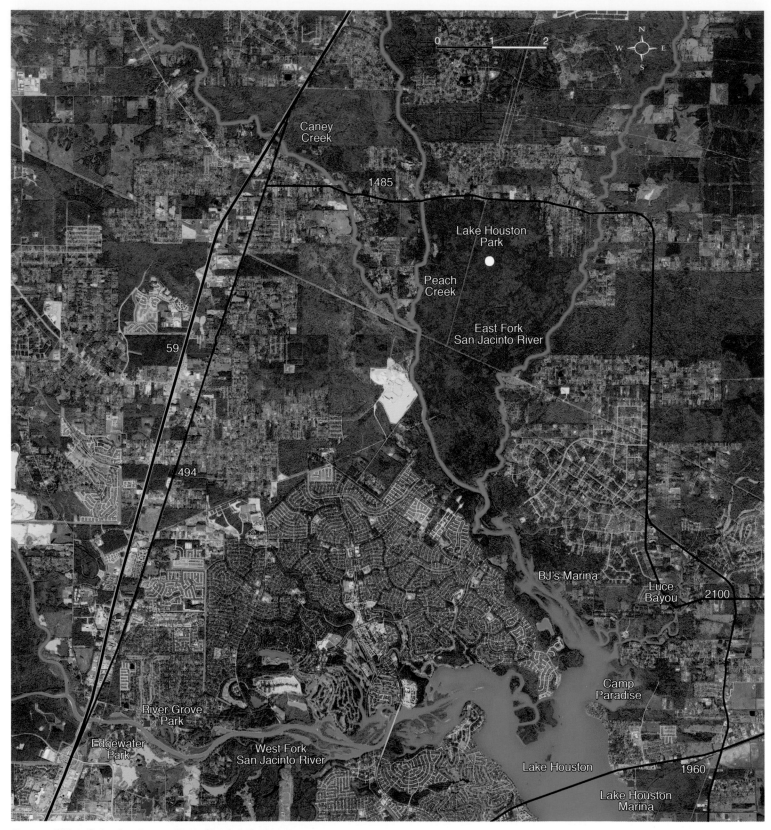

Caney
Creek

1485

Lake Houston
Park

Peach
Creek

East Fork
San Jacinto River

59

494

BJ's Marina

Luce
Bayou

2100

Camp
Paradise

River Grove
Park

Edgewater
Park

West Fork
San Jacinto River

Lake Houston

1960

Lake Houston
Marina

East and West forks, San Jacinto River, North Lake Houston

road to access Loop 494 southbound (another right turn), do so and proceed south on 494 to Hamblen Road (you may be forced to make this turn). Travel east on Hamblen Road to its end, following the right bend in the road toward the water or left to the launching area.

River Grove Park is a private park for Kingwood residents only, so the put-in is available only if you or a friend has a resident pass. This is a lovely spot to take off for exploring upstream on the West Branch of the San Jacinto or the upper reaches of Lake Houston. You could potentially link this to BJ's Marina or Camp Paradise if you want to run a shuttle. The northern shores are pretty much undisturbed and in a natural state, although, like any area close to Houston, housing pressure is on and new homes are being built along the lake.

Peach Creek

Peach Creek is a spring-fed perennial stream that forms one side of a boundary for Lake Houston State Park. It flows through woodlands for almost its entire length. Although paddleable, it is also prone to multiple obstructions from downed trees. The current recommended approach is from Lake Houston, paddling upstream against the current. Its upper source can be accessed from Lake Houston State Park, but anticipate spending a lot of time dodging trees and logjams.

Access 1: Lake Houston Park

➡ *Directions.* To reach Lake Houston Park, take FM 1485 about 2 miles east from the town of New Caney to Baptist Encampment Road. Travel south on Baptist Encampment Road for about 1.5 miles to Lake Houston State Park. The road past the office goes to the Peach Creek Bridge. You may park your vehicle there for as long as 15 minutes to offload your boat but must then move to another parking place. To the right of the bridge is a trail leading to a beach that affords easy creek access. The park was transferred to the City of Houston in 2006 and is under development that may result in improved river/creek access in the future. Day use of the park costs $3.

Lake Houston Park, located at the confluence of Caney Creek and the East Fork of the San Jacinto River, covers almost 5,000 acres. Some 200 acres of this site are the former Peach Creek Girl Scout Camp, which was added to the park in 1990. In 2006 the seventh annual San Jacinto Adventure Canoe and Kayak Race started here at 5:00 a.m. with a mad quarter-mile dash by the racers carrying their boats from the start to the water.

If you are running the 16-mile race, paddle downstream from here to the junction with Caney Creek; continue downstream to the East Fork of the San Jacinto River; cross Lake Houston to the West Fork of the San Jacinto; and then paddle upstream to the finish at River Grove Park in Kingwood. The race is put on by the San Jacinto Conservation Coalition (www.sanjacinto.cc/index.htm).

Access 2: BJ's Marina, Lake Houston

➡ *Directions.* From the intersection of FM 1960 and FM 2100, drive north on 2100. Follow it for 2.4 miles; at the intersection with Huffman Cleveland Road, go left and travel 1.4 miles. At the intersection with Magnolia Point Drive, turn left and follow the road 1.1 miles. Just after the left bend in the road, make a slight right onto Cheatham Road. Follow Cheatham Road one-fourth mile, and turn left on Calvin Road. BJ's address is 27907 Calvin Road, Huffman (281-324-9199).

This is an alternative, for-fee put-in ($3 per boat in January 2009) with direct access to Lake Houston. A memorable Houston Canoe Club trip put in here after dark and paddled a mile or so upstream to a suitable island to have a moonlight snack and visit. It was a fun, different kind of trip. This also has potential as a takeout for a West Fork of the San Jacinto River trip that might put in from the 1485 crossing of Peach Creek or Caney Creek.

Luce Bayou

This beautiful, clean, clear bayou comes into Lake Houston at its northeastern corner. The distance from here to its origin north of Dayton is 23 miles, but I

Enjoying Peach Creek and its large sandbar, Lake Houston Park

have paddled only 5 or so miles of its length closest to Lake Houston. When I paddled it last, there were huge cypress trees in and next to the water, and all of the upper regions were completely shaded by large trees. Unfortunately, that same day bulldozers and saws were at work clearing the land adjoining the bayou, presumably for more development, so I do not know how much of the pristine tall forest remains. Because duckweed covered the surface of the water, canoes

left swirled tracks in their wake. We paddled around an island and practiced "log jumping," getting out of the boats to lift them over giant logs across the bayou.

There are at least three places to access Luce Bayou—all require an out-and-back trip.

Access 1: Camp Paradise
➡ *Directions.* To reach this commercial, for-fee access, from Houston take US 59 north, turn right

onto FM 1960, cross the lake, and turn left onto FM 2100. Turn left on Cry Baby Lane (before Huffman Cleveland Road). Cry Baby is not an all-weather road, so beware if it's been raining. From Camp Paradise, follow the shoreline to your right (north) and then northeast into Luce Bayou.

While paddling here, enjoy the still, quiet waters and the tall cypress trees.

Access 2: FM 2100

➡ *Directions.* From FM 1960 east of Lake Houston, head north on FM 2100. You will cross Luce Bayou 3.5 miles from the 1960/2100 intersection. You can access the bayou from the right-of-way from FM 2100.

You can explore both upstream and downstream from here.

Access 3: Ponderosa Marina

➡ *Directions.* From FM 1960 east of Lake Houston, head north on FM 2100. At the intersection with Huffman Cleveland Road, turn left (west). About three-fourths mile down the road, just before it crosses the bayou, there is a large gravel parking lot and a boat ramp on your right. This is the Ponderosa Marina, a self-pay private launch facility right on the bayou. Cost is $7 per car plus $3 per person for everyone except the driver. Call 281-450-0342 for more information.

A relatively short paddle downstream takes you to Lake Houston; upstream you can go for several miles though the tall trees until you run out of enough water to float your boat or maneuver through the trees.

East Fork, San Jacinto River

➡ *Directions.* From Lake Houston Parkway, east of Beltway 8 (Sam Houston Parkway), travel west to Deussen Parkway (about 3 miles east of Beltway 8). Turn left (north) on Deussen Parkway, and travel about a mile to Deussen Drive; turn left on Somnier Drive to the boat ramp. This puts you on Lake Houston; there is no access to the downstream San Jacinto River from this park.

Cindy and John Bartos leading a Houston Canoe Club trip on a side slough of the East Fork of the San Jacinto River

Barely mentioned in the *Analysis of Texas Waterways,* the East Fork carries much less water than the West Fork of the San Jacinto. It is a lovely day paddle with tall pine, cypress, and oak woods. River birch is predominant on the upstream islands (from BJ's Marina) and a good place to see red maple first emerging in early spring. Paddling north from BJ's, you will reach the southern tip of (as yet undeveloped) Lake Houston Park. There are lovely side channels, but note

▲ *Lower stretches of Luce Bayou. Photo by Joe Coker*

▲▶ *Where the cypress trees touch overhead on Luce Bayou. Photo by Joe Coker*

that much of the property is private and is specifically posted "for owners only."

At the south end of Lake Houston, access via Alexander Deussen Park. Expect wind, waves, and motorboats. There is a public boat ramp at the far southern end of Lake Houston on its western shore. Be sure to make yourself visible to the motorfolks; they are not used to looking for craft of our size and are a lot bigger, heavier, and faster than we are.

San Jacinto River below Lake Houston

Eisenhower Park, located at 13400 Aqueduct Road in Houston, affords access to the San Jacinto River from the parking lot and picnic area at Big Eddy. You

will have to carry your boat about 100 yards to the water. You won't be able to paddle far upstream on the river; be sure to note how much current there is before you decide on a downstream and then upstream return route. About 4 miles downstream, there is a for-fee ($10 per boat in 2011) access point at Love's Marina on US Business 90, which is a popular place for Jet Ski access as well, so expect a lot of that traffic in warm weather. Rio Villa Park, 11 miles downstream of Eisenhower Park, has a very nice canoe ramp and river access. Wallisville Road (east of Beltway 8) stops at the access road to the park (Rio Villa Drive), where you make a hard left turn and go about another half mile to the end of the road and the parking area. You will note good potential access

the Turning Basin. Availing yourself of the Rio Villa Park is a good choice; points farther south are not recommended.

Cypress Creek

Cypress Creek is a tributary to the San Jacinto River that joins it at Lake Houston. This beautiful unchannelized stream has several paddleable segments. It is also heavily wooded, so be on the lookout for trees that are down in the water or just above the surface. Canoeists call tree branches in the water "strainers." Like the cooking utensil, they will strain the solid items (you and your canoe) from the liquid (the creek). At best this is uncomfortable; at worst, it can be deadly, so if you do not have good maneuvering skills, you may want to leave at least the upper stretches alone and the bottom ones when the river is up and the current racing. At low-water levels (especially too low for paddling), there are beautiful big white sandbars, which may or may not be visible at higher water levels.

Most of the year there isn't enough water to make the upper runs, so check the gaging stations before you decide whether or not to paddle. Your other pretrip arrangement should be to call Mercer Arboretum (281-443-8731) if you plan to use the canoe ramp there for either putting in or taking out; or call Jesse Jones Park (281-446-8588), located at a point after Cypress Creek joins Spring Creek.

Access 1: Meyer Park
➡ *Directions.* Meyer Park is located at 7700 Cypresswood Drive in Spring. From Stuebner Airline Road, turn west on Cypresswood. The park appears on both sides of the road; you want to drive in to the south part of the park to unload your boats and gear. If there's enough water to paddle the stream, this will not work well as an out-and-back trip, so arrange a shuttle for the distance you want to paddle downstream. The park has a large sports complex, thus nice restroom facilities, and hiking/jogging trails.

Cypresswood Park is not very far downstream and could be an alternate put-in or very short distance

points also from Wallisville Road before it gets to Rio Villa. From the large paved parking area at the park, you will have to carry your boat at least 200 yards to the ramp; I would suggest bringing wheels for your canoe if you want to put in or take out here.

Some miles below Rio Villa Park, the river flows under I-10. From here the river is highly industrialized as it approaches its intersection with Buffalo Bayou and shortly thereafter the Lynchburg Ferry crossing. Unfortunately, the Buffalo Bayou/Houston Ship Channel is closed to private boats upstream of the San Jacinto Monument State Historic Park. Security Zones for the Houston Ship Channel start just upstream of the Battleship *Texas* and continue for all of the Buffalo Bayou/Ship Channel upstream to at least

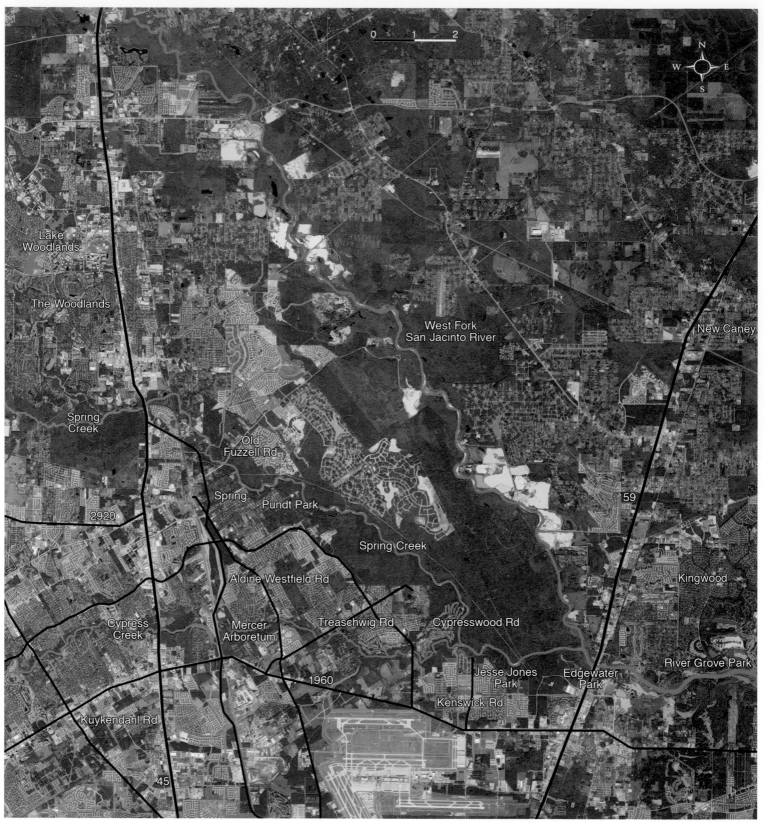

Spring and Cypress Creeks

take-out; 4 miles from Meyer Park is the Kuykendahl Road crossing; or for a much longer paddle, Mercer Arboretum is 12 miles downstream (8 miles from Kuykendahl).

Access 2: Kuykendahl Road Crossing

There is a "no motor vehicles" sign posted on the northeastern corner of the crossing. That is the spot to carry your craft down to or up from the river. To be safe, you should probably park away from the crossing and well off the side of the shoulders of the road. If this is your put-in, make sure you have contacted—well in advance—Mercer Arboretum (281-443-8731) if you plan to use its boat landing area for a take-out. Mercer is located 8 miles downstream, so you don't want to find out you can't take out there when you arrive on the spot. Cypress Creek near here has been built up, but there are fewer and fewer signs of development as you head downstream. Like the previous segment, beware of low water and/or strainers in the water. You will see more and more of the namesake cypress trees as you continue along. You will be crossing under I-45 and the Hardy Toll Road. Immediately after the toll road is a railroad crossing that you may wish to portage (carry around). Slow down there, and look before you leap or get into a situation that could be very dangerous. When you approach the Aldine Westfield Bridge, look for the trail to the take-out on your right. You scouted for it and noted its location when you ran your shuttle, didn't you?

Access 3: Mercer Arboretum

Mercer Arboretum is located at 22306 Aldine Westfield Road in Houston; the canoe launch is on the opposite side of Aldine Westfield Road from the arboretum. You need to call 281-443-8731 to make sure you can use the put-in/take-out. The bank is a quite steep sandbar, so you may want to scout it before you decide to try to put in here.

I am very fond of gardening, and of all the public gardens around Houston, this is my favorite. This may be a good lure for shuttle drivers who otherwise don't want to join you on the stream, and if I'm on a trip in the vicinity, I will be sure to find time to walk through the gardens and down the woodland trail to the iris pond, Japanese pagoda, and bamboo display. I go there as often as I can to enjoy a wide variety of plants in bloom every month of the year, to see which plants are featured and how they are managed, pruned, and displayed. The restroom is available when the center is open. Jesse Jones Park is 6 miles downstream, after Cypress Creek has joined Spring Creek. Be sure to call Jesse Jones Park (281-446-8588) to be able to use the facilities there.

Spring Creek

When I was researching historical information on Spring Creek, I was amused to see how many Spring Creeks there are in Texas. This one was also known as Arroyo de Santa Rosa del Alcazar and starts in northeastern Waller County. It forms the northern boundary between Waller and Harris, and Montgomery and

Canoeists enjoying a break on a large sandbar on Cypress Creek during a trip run by the Jesse Jones Nature Center, January 2008

Harris counties. As the name implies, it has long been fed by springs along its length, and early Native Americans camped on its banks before Europeans ever came this way. Remnants of hardwood forests line its length; a series of parks are planned to make the stream more accessible and preserve its beauty. The Spring Creek Greenway Project targets 12,000 acres along the creek as a nature preserve and outdoor recreation facility. Some of the sand for the beaches in Galveston, and indeed along the Gulf of Mexico, come from streams like this, as well as rivers, bayous, and creeks. The sandbars are beautiful and numerous. You should find one to your liking for a lunch or snack stop.

Access 1: Old Riley Fuzzell Road Crossing

➔ *Directions.* Drive north on Aldine Westfield Road from the Mercer Arboretum to a T-intersection. Turn right and cross under the Hardy Toll Road. Stop where the road crosses Spring Creek, carefully park your car, and walk your canoe and gear down to the creek.

The canoe launch was improved and dedicated to the public in April 2007. Currently you need to park at the barricade at the end of the older section of Riley Fuzzell Road to access the launch. You can take a short trip of 2.8 miles to Pundt Park downstream or a longer 11-mile trip to Jesse Jones Park and Nature Center. If the latter is your destination, you must arrange a shuttle in advance and permission to use the Jesse Jones Park canoe launch for a takeout (281-446-8588). Make sure Spring Creek water flow will support your trip; this is a *very* long way to have to drag your canoe or kayak over sandbars if the water is too low, a situation that happens with some frequency.

Access 2: Pundt Park

Pundt Park was opened in 2010 some 2.5 miles downstream of the Riley Fuzzell launch. It provides a primitive canoe launch (no improvements, just access to the stream). It also has picnic facilities, restrooms, and a trailhead for the walking trail of the Spring Creek Greenway. Hart Lake and Heron Pond are here, too, but canoeing and kayaking are prohibited on them.

It is 8.3 miles from here to Jesse Jones Park. Call Pundt Park (281-353-4196) for more information or reservations.

Access 3: Jesse Jones Park and Nature Center

Jesse Jones Park and Nature Center is located at 20634 Kenswick Drive in Humble. To be sure the park will be open, and the boat ramp accessible when you arrive, call 281-446-8588. This park offers many activities for family members or friends who may or may not want to participate in the canoe trip. If you would rather go with a pro before you shove off to do this trip on your own, there are staff-guided pontoon boat rides from the park and staff-guided canoe trips on Spring Creek. Both activities require reservations at least 10 days in advance. Be sure to visit the park's Web site for other activities (www.hcp4.net/jones/). There are nice playgrounds and restroom facilities available.

If you would like to use this as a put-in rather than a take-out, you can paddle downstream about 4 miles to where Spring Creek joins the San Jacinto River and take out by the US 59 bridge at Edgewater Park.

Access 4: Edgewater Park

➔ *Directions.* From Jesse Jones Park, head south on Kenswick Drive to FM 1960/FM 1960 Bypass. Turn left on FM 1960 Bypass, and travel 1.7 miles. At the intersection with the Eastex Freeway (US 59), go north on 59 for 1.8 miles. The highway map I consulted makes the next step look rather complicated. Take the first exit north of the 59 crossing of the San Jacinto, and make your way south until you are almost under the bridge. It doesn't appear that an access road crosses the river.

Lake Woodlands

➔ *Directions.* Northshore Park, on Lake Woodlands Drive, provides direct access to Lake Woodlands. Traveling north on I-45, take Exit 77 (Woodlands Parkway), but stay on the frontage road to circle around and use the overpass to Lake Woodlands Drive about a half mile from Woodlands Parkway. As you are westbound on Lake Woodlands Drive, look for the park on your left.

Panther Branch of Spring Creek is dammed to form Lake Woodlands in the master-planned community of The Woodlands. Although the lake is only a few miles in length, fast motorcraft are banned in at least the upper regions. Northshore Park provides easy access to the water, and good restroom and playground facilities make this a pleasant place to put a boat in the water. The upper stretches of Lake Woodlands are very much in a natural state, or you can paddle south to see the built-up sections. Bald eagles have been reported at the northern edge of the lake. The park is gated, however, so be sure to get back to your car before dark so you are not locked in.

Greens Bayou

➡ *Directions*. To get to Greens Bayou Park at 700 Westmont Drive, exit I-10 east of downtown Houston at the Uvalde exit. Head west on the frontage road to Westmont Street. Travel north on Westmont about half a mile. Greens Bayou Park will be on your left. This is an unimproved park with free public access to Greens Bayou.

Greens Bayou Park gives nice access to the water. From there you can paddle upstream for several miles to US 90. Buyouts of flooded properties from Tropical Storm Allison and additional property acquisitions will create more of a greenbelt along Greens Bayou, including Coolgreen Park farther south from Greens Bayou Park. Maxey Park, a dog park, offers good potential access to the water. Several miles farther upstream, the 1,200-acre Greens Bayou wetland mitigation bank should help improve the quality of the water in Greens Bayou and help in flood control.

This is a slow-moving bayou, some parts with tall pine trees, and others with young cypress trees. Its urban setting is belied by kingfisher birds, great blue herons, and American egrets. The paddle upstream is easy.

Greens Bayou Corridor Coalition is working to create a major linear park and trail system to interconnect and serve the Greens Bayou Corridor communities and improve the local environment and water quality. Look forward to improved access and facilities in the future.

Buffalo Bayou

Buffalo Bayou has played an important role in the development of the city of Houston and continues as a natural focus for quality of life and parkland for the city. In my twenty-five years in the Houston area, developing the bayou as a greenbelt has been dramatic and is ongoing as of the publication of this book. The bayou rises west of Katy in Fort Bend County and flows 65 miles east to its mouth on the San Jacinto River at Lynchburg. Major tributaries are White Oak Bayou, in downtown Houston; Brays Bayou, just downstream of the Turning Basin of the Houston Ship Channel; then Sims, Hunting, and Greens bayous; and finally the San Jacinto River.

Where White Oak Bayou joins Buffalo Bayou, Augustus and John Allen purchased property in August 1836 to develop a town plat for Houston and promoted it as the seat of Texas government. Houston did not persist as the capital, but it grew and prospered as a trading center with water connections to Galveston. In 1914 the lower reaches of the bayou were dredged to a depth of 25 feet to form the Houston Ship Channel and to 30 feet in 1930; it is currently under negotiation and development to increase the depth from its current 50 feet to 75 feet. The Turning Basin, the head of navigation for large ships, is off limits to canoes and kayaks per post-9/11 security measures. Master plans for Buffalo Bayou include development of a 2,500-acre park system from Memorial Park to the Turning Basin. Heavy industrialization of the Ship Channel portion of Buffalo Bayou resulted in pollution of the waterway, but through legislation and regulation it is rebounding; upper stretches of the bayou include heavily wooded stretches through River Oaks and Memorial Park, belying its location within the city limits. The downtown section of the bayou is crisscrossed by bridges, including very heavily traveled I-45, US 59, and many other crossings.

Greens Bayou

Texas Parks and Wildlife Department recently designated Buffalo Bayou as a Coastal Paddle Trail. Its Web site includes a map and estimated paddle times between access points. For an armchair trip down the bayou and great background information, see Geoff Winningham's book *Along Forgotten River: Photographs of Buffalo Bayou and the Houston Ship Channel, 1997–2001, with Accounts of Early Travelers to Texas 1767–1858.* Louis Aulbach's *Buffalo Bayou, an Echo of Houston's Wilderness Beginnings* is an excellent history of the bayou.

Upstream of TX 6, the bayou flows through George Bush Park. An unfortunate incident with a lost kayaker in the Bush Park area resulted in closing of this section of the bayou to paddlers, so my descriptions will start downstream of the TX 6 crossing. Flood gates at the park control the level of the upstream bayou and help control flooding in periods of high rainfall. Releases from the dam control downstream levels, with a baseline flow of about 200 cfs (cubic feet per second) on the downtown gage. The bayou is tidally influenced at least as far as White Oak Bayou, so there are a multitude of environmental factors you should check out before disembarking. In the upper reaches the downstream flow is quite noticeable. Depending on tides, lower stretches can have an upstream flow. Out-and-back trips are doable on many stretches.

Access 1: TX 6 Crossing

On the northwestern corner of this intersection is a nice parking lot. Access to the bayou, however, is across concrete that is potentially very slippery if it is wet. Proceed with extreme caution. The current is rather swift here, so it is not a recommended put-in if you are unsure of your footing or in any way uncertain of your boat-handling skills. You are very close to where water is released from Barker Dam immediately upstream.

Under the TX 6 bridge and barely downstream is a concrete block, complete with riprap that can tear a hole in your boat. A less dangerous access point is about 1.0 to 1.5 miles downstream, approaching from the north side of the bayou at Terry Hershey Park.

Access 2: Hershey Park at Memorial Mews

➡ *Directions. Directions.* Take Memorial Mews south from Memorial Drive to its end. Unload there, and walk boats and gear down to the water. Wilcrest bridge at the Boheme and Wycliffe intersection is 5 miles downstream. From the put-in you will need to float about 100 yards on a side channel of Buffalo Bayou to the main bayou, and you are on your way.

The first bridge you reach is Eldridge Parkway. Turkey Creek enters very soon from the left bank. You may want to eddy out here to paddle upstream for a closer look. Turkey Creek's contribution to Buffalo Bayou includes some rocks and riffles just downstream, so keep your eyes peeled for obstructions. In another mile or so, where the Dairy Ashford bridge crosses the bayou, is an alternative put-in or take-out with a parking area on the southeastern bank. Lakeside Country Club tops the embankment to the right as you approach the Wilcrest bridge; your take-out includes the steps immediately beyond the bridge. The distance from the second access point is about 5 miles.

Nonpaddling members of your group can enjoy 12 miles of hiking trails, bikeways, and people- and dog-watching in Terry Hershey Park. There are playgrounds, restrooms, and drinking fountains for people and dogs throughout the park. Terry Hershey Park includes the banks of the bayou from TX 6 to Beltway 8 (Sam Houston Parkway).

Access 3: Terry Hershey Park at Wilcrest

There is no parking available right at the Wilcrest crossing; and as noted previously, you will have to navigate a set of steps to get to the water. You can unload your gear at the trailhead, on the northeastern corner of Wilcrest bridge, and then move your vehicle. For parking, head north on Wilcrest, turn right at the first street (Indian Creek), turn right again on Wycliff/ Boheme, and park where you can. Then walk back down to the bayou.

This stretch of the bayou has the closest thing to whitewater in Houston, a nice Class I+ riffle at Briar Bend, and some warm-up maneuvers before you get there. You will encounter a waterfall feature and pipe

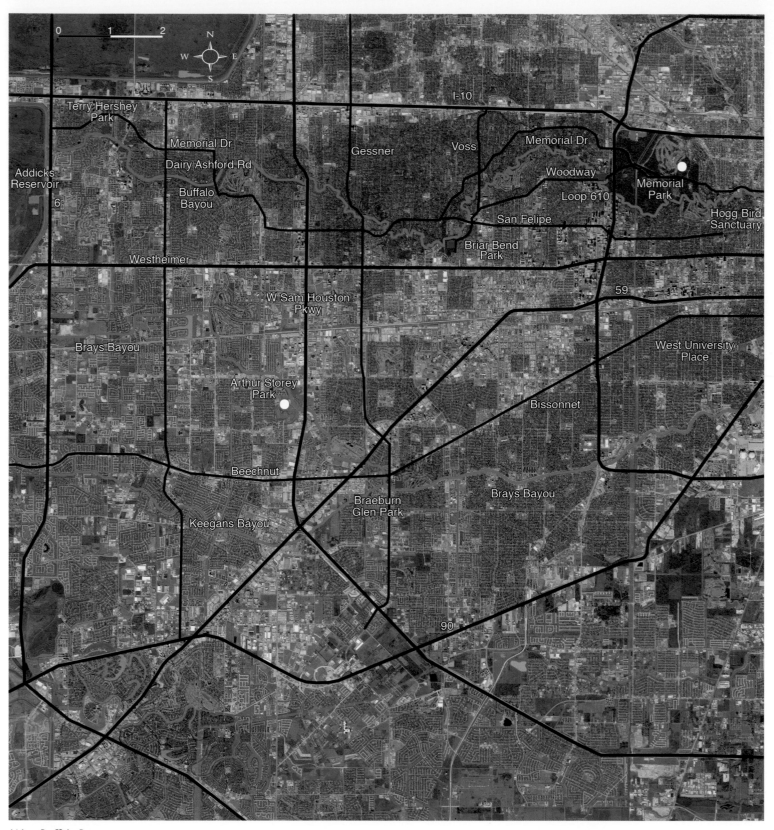

West Buffalo Bayou

Buffalo Bayou in downtown Houston

crossings where the pipe may be at, above, or below the water level, so beware. This 6-mile stretch has multiple bridge crossings: Beltway 8, Gessner, Briar Forest, Piney Point. This is one of the few places on streams in or around Houston where you see some actual rock outcrops—almost all other streams seem to have mud or sand bottoms. You will also observe several different attempts to control stream erosion and conserve the bank. The water course is heavily forested with large trees along the way, including sycamores and other hardwoods.

There is no obvious bridge to mark the take-out (or put-in) at Briar Bend Park, so by all means, when you park a shuttle car here, walk down to the water and make sure you recognize what it will look like from the water. This is always a good idea, but particularly important when there are no readily identifiable features (like bridges) that keep you from overrunning where you intend to stop!

Access 4: Briar Bend Park

➡ *Directions.* To reach the park, go north on Stoney Brook from its intersection with Westheimer. From the stop sign at the intersection with Woodway, turn left. Where the street makes an abrupt left turn, park and look for the trail heading down to the water, which may be as much as 40 to 50 feet below the street level. Houston Canoe Club and Bayou Preservation Association have maintained this put-in on a periodic basis, so be prepared for whatever comes your way. Your next available take-out is 6 miles downstream at the western edge of Memorial Park, right next to the Woodway bridge.

San Felipe is the first bridge across the bayou, followed in approximately another mile by Voss. The Houston Country Club extends along the south side of the bayou for a mile and half beginning a half mile or so beyond Voss; Hunters Creek Village is to the north. There is an actual riffle/rapid on this stretch, shortly before the Chimney Rock crossing and about 4 miles into your paddle—keep an eye/ear on the alert so you don't get a surprise. The next major road crossing is Woodway. A gentler canoe launch/take-out is supposedly in the works, but the last time I paddled from Woodway, we parked on the south side of its crossing the bayou, on the west side of the road, and had to negotiate a fairly steep bank to the bayou. It's a good idea to scout this carefully when you park a shuttle car here and find the most benign place to take your canoe out of the water—or to put it in for the next stretch.

Access 5: Woodway Crossing

From here you will paddle through River Oaks, which has some of the nicest backyards in all of Houston (and upstream isn't so bad, either). I am suggesting Eleanor Tinsley Park as your take-out downstream. That makes this stretch at least 8 miles in length. I found out to my chagrin that a host of Girl Scouts take much longer than 5 hours to paddle this stretch, including a lunch break; and they were pretty tired afterward. Watch the water level (the day the Scouts paddled, the level was not particularly low), and allow plenty of time. This is not a good choice for your first paddle trip.

Memorial Park, which flanks the bayou on both sides for the first several miles, was actually an army camp (Camp Logan) for a short time around World War I. Houston Arboretum is on the south side of the bayou; if you have time to visit, you will get a good look at what Houston probably looked like before the city rose from the banks of the bayou. A pedestrian bridge crosses the bayou between the Hogg Bird Sanctuary and Bayou Bend Gardens and Museum. The gardens are a frequent feature of the spring Azalea Trail, and if you enjoy beautiful antique furniture, the museum is well worth the visit. A little farther downstream is the Rainbow Lodge, one of Houston's well-known eateries, but you won't feel comfortable here dressed in canoeing gear.

Access 6: Hogg Bird Sanctuary

This is a relatively new access point and shares the parking lot at 1 Westcott Street with the Bayou Bend

mansion. There has been some controversy about whether or not canoe access here is disturbing to the birds or violates the sanctity of an avian retreat, so you may or may not want to access the creek here by way of a long trail to the water. However, as an intermediate take-out to the otherwise very long trip to Eleanor Tinsley Park from the Woodway access, it is very desirable.

Access 7: Eleanor Tinsley Park

Eleanor Tinsley Park, located at 500 Allen Parkway, has good but small parking lot and some of the nicest views of downtown Houston, from water level or from the level of the parking lot. The park is accessed from Allen Parkway westbound just east of the Sabine Street bridge. You will need a good city map and/or a knowledgeable navigator on board to locate the park. The Buffalo Bayou Regatta races use this as their ending point. It's a lot more fun putting boats into the water here than taking out—and again the launch is downstream (toward the downtown area) of the parking area, probably 200 yards away. You will find that boats slide downhill quite nicely on grass.

Access 8: Sabine Street Canoe Launch

Several organizations have worked together to update and beautify the banks of the bayou, particularly in the Sabine-to-Bagby Promenade and Buffalo Bayou Walk. On the north side of the bayou is a small parking lot and a path down to the bayou to facilitate canoe/kayak launching. This is only a quarter mile downstream of Eleanor Tinsley Park, and perhaps a half mile from the Main Street crossing. If you have time, walk the bayou banks here and enjoy the artwork and view, or perhaps you are participating in one of the many activities the Buffalo Bayou Partnership is sponsoring.

Access 9: Allen's Landing Park/Main Street Crossing

There is a for-pay parking lot right behind the Spaghetti Warehouse at 901 Commerce Street. Cost was $3 per car in 2010, and a pasta dinner is a fun way to end a trip. It's not a dress-up place, so canoe casual

Classic view of downtown Houston from Buffalo Bayou, just downstream of Eleanor-Tinsley Park

works; just leave your muddy sneakers in the car. This is only about a half mile downstream of Tinsley Park. Between the two are a multitude of road crossings of I-45, access roads, and McKinney, Rusk, Memorial, Bagby, Preston, Congress, Franklin, Louisiana, and Milam streets. Obviously, there are a lot of them, and as you would expect, many pillars supporting the elevated roadways. In my opinion this stretch cries

out for a giant slalom race utilizing all those concrete markers already in place!

During the past thirty years, since I first paddled this stretch, the bayou environs have dramatically improved; you can expect this to continue for some time as the Buffalo Bayou Partnership develops this part of the Buffalo Bayou corridor. The partnership's authority includes a 2,500-acre park system that extends from

Natural stretch of Buffalo Bayou in the downtown area of Houston

Shepherd Drive and Memorial Park to the Turning Basin. Under development are Buffalo Bend Park next to the Turning Basin (the upper limit of navigation of Buffalo Bayou by oceangoing vessels and off limits to private boaters, as is the length of the Houston Ship Channel/Buffalo Bayou as far downstream as San Jacinto State Park) and Tony Marron Park (at North York). No fewer than twelve portals/access points are or will be developed. Walking trails will be developed as well. Watch the renovation of warehouses to living space and new condos and townhouses springing up all along these stretches of bayou.

Another interesting way to use the Main Street crossing access point is as a base for out-and-back trips; upstream to Tinsley Park or immediately downstream is Allen's Landing Park, the site of the Allen brothers' development of Houston at the intersection of White Oak Bayou and Buffalo Bayou.

At the time of this writing, Main Street is the farthest downstream access that is developed. Next below the proposed Buffalo Bend Park is the Turning Basin for the Houston Ship Channel.

Brays Bayou

Brays Bayou (see the map of West Buffalo Bayou) runs west to east just south of Buffalo Bayou, which it joins to form the Houston Ship Channel. Like Buffalo Bayou, it drains some of the most expensive real estate in Houston, including the Texas Medical Center, Houston Zoo, Hermann Park, Houston Baptist University, Rice University, Texas Southern University, and University of Houston. During Tropical Storm Allison the floodwaters from Brays and Buffalo bayous damaged many of those locations. Brays Bayou has a history of flooding from the beginning of the settlement of Houston, for which it has been channelized, concreted, and denuded of much of its woodland for most of its 31-mile length. The middle stretches have so many human-made alterations that it is rendered particularly dangerous in anything but the mildest flows, so only two stretches are desirable for paddling at this time. Like many of our area's water bodies, there is hope for its future. According to HCFCD, Project Brays is under way as the "most significant flood damage reduction initiative ever to be managed by Harris County Flood Control District." Its partners include the US Army Corps of Engineers, and local groups whose objective is also to bring greenspace and recreational amenities to the communities along the bayou—Bellaire, Houston, Southside Place, West University Place, Meadows Place, and Missouri City.

Brays Bayou hike-and-bike trails provide land-based enjoyment of the bayou. The following descriptions are excerpted from Eric Ruckstuhl's canoeing trails' listing at the Bayou Preservation Association Web site (www.bayoupreservation.org; click on "trails").

Brays Bayou Segment 1: Art Storey Park

This paddle is 3.5 miles long. You must leave your canoe or kayak at Bellaire Boulevard's intersection with the bayou and move your car to the parking lot on Beltway 8; or better yet, get a friend to take your car to Braeburn Glen Park to eliminate the problem of running a shuttle. The bayou will take you under

Beltway 8 and US 59. The next bridge after 59 is Braeburn Glen Boulevard, where you will take out at Braeburn Glen Park. Unfortunately, the banks are concreted from 59 to this point, so you will have to scramble up those steep, and potentially very slippery, banks to get yourself and your boat off the bayou. Eric Ruckstuhl describes a set of steps on the left bank, just past the Braeburn Glen bridge.

Brays Bayou Segment 2: MacGregor Park to Mason Park

This paddle is 5 miles long. Because of fencing in MacGregor Park, access to the bayou is from the right-of-way of M. L. King Boulevard, described as a difficult access; as for the first segment, if you are leaving a vehicle at this end, you will need to move it to a legitimate parking spot within MacGregor Park. Be sure to have a good street map with you, as you will need to count bridges and make sure to look for Mason Park, after the 75th Street bridge, and after you have gone under MLK, railroad, OST, South Wayside, Telephone, Lawndale, and Forest Hill overpasses. The take-out spot is on the right bank of the bayou.

Sims Bayou

➡ *Directions.* The put-in for the stretch described is at Reveille Park. To get there from I-45 (Gulf Freeway), take the Bellfort/Howard Street exit. Travel west on Bellfort (its name is Howard to the east of I-45 and Bellfort to the west) about 1.3 miles to the intersection with Telephone Road (TX 35). Turn right (north) at this intersection, but stay in the right lane, as the road forks in a short distance. Bear right on what is now Reveille Street. Shortly you will reach Vista Verde and then Oak Vista. You can turn right on either of these streets to Reveille Park. The best put-in is from Vista Verde, but you will have to move your car to the parking lot on Oak Vista if you are leaving a car at this park. It's a long carry over the bank and down to the bayou, so be prepared.

The take-out is at Milby Park. To get there from Reveille Park, drive north eight blocks on Joplin Street

(forms the west side boundary of the park) to Park Place Boulevard. Turn right (east) on Park Place; cross under the Gulf Freeway and north on Broadway. Turn right (east) eleven blocks farther north (the next street north after Brockton) on Park Terrace, cross Old Galveston Road (TX 3) and the railroad tracks, and you are now on Central Street. In about a half mile the sign for Milby Park will be on your right. Turn in and park by the big oak trees and the permanent building. There is no path from the bayou here, so note the location carefully so you won't paddle past it. If you run a shuttle and leave a car here, you can paddle one way from Reveille instead of an out-and-back trip from either location.

Sims Bayou runs south and east of Loop 610 and empties into the Buffalo Bayou/Houston Ship Channel along one of its most industrialized stretches. Samuel Ezekiel Allen built a ranch house near the mouth of Sims Bayou at Buffalo Bayou in the late 1800s and owned between 10,000 and 20,000 acres in this area at his death in 1913. Some small parcels of natural riverbank and streambed remain after multiple efforts of the USACE to channelize the bayou and control its flooding. A Sims Bayou Recreation Plan was authorized along with flood damage reduction projects.

Although the bayou is 117 miles in length, a lot of it is channelized with treeless banks. The stretch described here is about 5 miles total, if you take both meander channels. The USGS maintains two gages on Sims Bayou; one (08075400) at the Hiram Clarke crossing; and the other (08075500) at Telephone Road.

■ *Paddling Note.* From the put-in, paddle downstream until the three golf cart bridges of Glenbrook Park municipal golf course come into view. Between the first and second bridges, on your left, is the opening into the first of the natural meanders. Sims Bayou Urban Nature Center backs up to this oxbow. There is a steep trail leading up to the nature center from the bayou. Paddling downstream from here, you will reach the main bayou again. Paddle upstream a short distance (to your right); then make a left turn onto the next natural meander. About halfway around this meander you will see Berry Creek enter—most notable

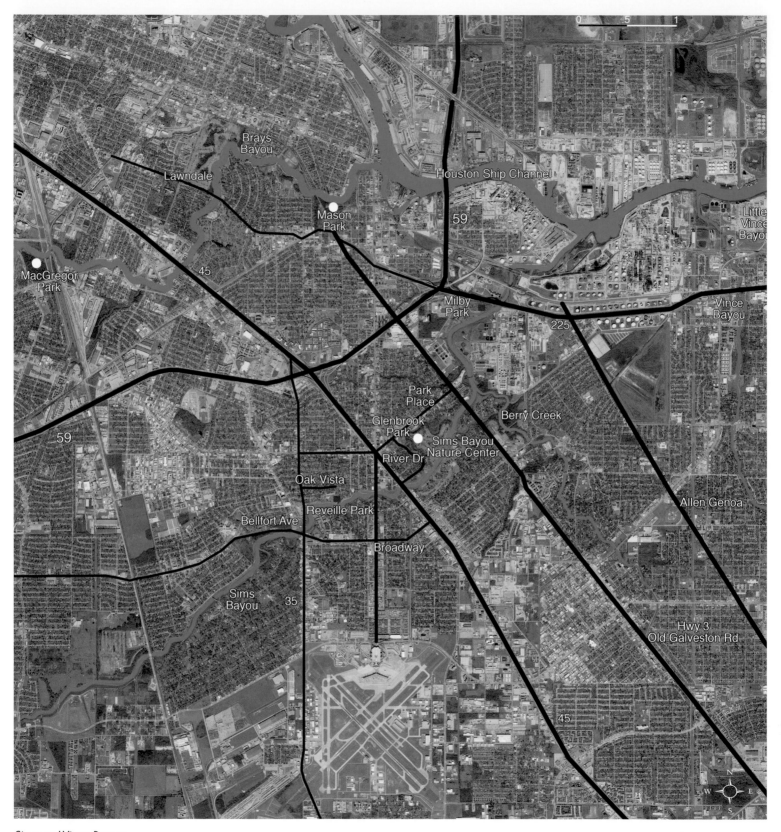

Sims and Vince Bayous

for the used-auto berm work apparently built by the landowner across the way trying to preserve his bank from Berry Creek in flood. When you reemerge on the main bayou, you will go right (still downstream) to Milby Park. You will have to crash through the underbrush that has grown up along the bayou until you are on the mowed lawns of Milby—this was the situation when I last paddled here. Enjoy a snack or meal under the big oak trees, and contemplate the bayou and the refineries beyond it. Not much farther downstream Sims Bayou empties into the Houston Ship Channel/Buffalo Bayou. That stretch is closed to private boat traffic, so don't miss the Milby Park take-out. TX 225 crosses Sims Bayou at the lower end of Milby Park and is a hard-to-miss landmark.

Vince Bayou

➡ *Directions.* Vince Bayou has only a short distance of bayou to paddle, but a very nice access point from Memorial Park in Pasadena. To get to Memorial Park, you can approach from the south side, eastbound access lanes of TX 225 or from West Jackson Street on its south end.

The two entry points don't appear to be connected; the one from West Jackson seems to be in closest proximity to the water. From here you can head out and back either upstream or downstream. You can paddle almost a mile downstream (i.e., north to the Houston Ship Channel) and about the same distance upstream. Just downstream of the 225 overpass is a sewage treatment plant; farther along is the junction with Little Vince Bayou, and then the Ship Channel, which is off limits to private boat traffic.

Gage 08075730 on Vince Bayou is located south of where Harris Avenue crosses the bayou, and even at that location shows tidal variations.

Sheldon Reservoir and Carpenters Bayou

➡ *Directions.* Sheldon Reservoir is easy to access with the completion of the Sam Houston Parkway. Take the Sam Houston Parkway (Beltway 8) about 8 miles

Sheldon Lake's face in summer—lilies in bloom and the water surface covered with vegetation

north of its intersection with I-10. Exit on Garrett Road, continue east (right turn from the parkway if you are going north) for about 200 yards, and turn right into the parking lot. If it is locked, retrace your route and take the first left onto Fauna (Pineland) Road. Follow it south to the boat ramp just north of US Business 90.

Sheldon Reservoir is an 800-acre lake constructed in 1942 by the federal government to provide water for war industries along the Houston Ship Channel. Texas Parks and Wildlife acquired the reservoir in 1952 and called it Sheldon Wildlife Management Area; it was opened in 1955. Sheldon Lake was designated a state park in 1984. The water for the lake comes from Carpenters Bayou, a tributary to Buffalo Bayou. Parts of the bayou directly upstream of the lake are natural and a lovely short paddle complete with water lilies and overhanging trees. In the right seasons of the year you can expect to see the lilies in bloom, hundreds of egrets and herons at their rookery, and lots

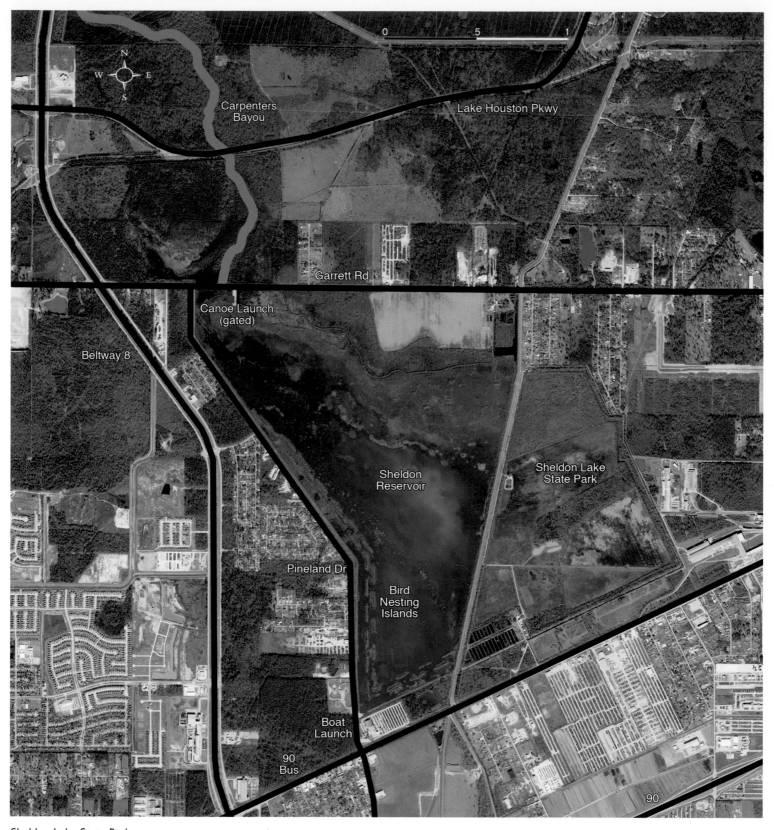

Sheldon Lake State Park

of alligators. The vegetation in the lake grows densely in warm weather. The lake is often impassable in the summer, but open in the winter.

The reservoir is generally closed to boat traffic from November 1 to March 1 to avoid disturbing water-fowl, but spring and early summer are fine before the various water plants clog the water. Call the park to be sure the water is open (281-456-2800). The lotus pads and stumps (and park regulations) limit the speed and number of powerboats. In the past we put our boats in the water at the parking lot off Garrett Road. Usually a number of alligators hang out around this put-in area, but if you don't harass them, they won't bother you. More recently the parking lot has been gated and locked, so you need to use the boat ramp on the southwestern corner of the lake, at the corner of Pineland Road and the south levee. Pineland Road also offers great viewing opportunities (with binoculars or a high-powered scope) of the bird rookeries. The Environmental Learning Center is on the south end of the property, off Business 90 (Old Beaumont Highway). From the Garth Road parking lot you can paddle south through the large lake and around the trees and hum-mocks, or you can paddle under the Garrett bridge and proceed north up Carpenters Bayou. Either route is good for several hours of adventure.

Sheldon Lake in winter showing that even then water hyacinth can be a problem

Facilities

San Jacinto River Basin

Paddling area	Access point	Toilet	Picnic	Camping	Water	Ramp	Parking	Gage	Mileage	Comments
Lake Conroe										
	Access 1: Stubblefield Recreation Area	•	•	•	•	•	•		10	Fee: Sam Houston National Forest
	Access 2: Scotts Ridge Recreation Area	•					•		10	
	Access 3: FM 830 ramp						•		10	
Lake Raven		•	•	•	•		•			Huntsville State Park
West Fork, San Jacinto River								08067650	18	
	TX 105 crossing								4	
	FM 2854 crossing								8	
	I-45 crossing								5	
	FM 242 crossing								18	
	Access 1: Edgewater Park						•	08068010	2	
	Access 2: River Grove Park									Private subdivision park
Peach Creek										
	Access 1: Lake Houston Park	•	•	•	•		•	08071000	10	Fee: Lake Houston Park
	Access 2: BJ's Marina, Lake Houston	•				•	•			Fee
	Caney Creek							08070500	10	
Luce Bayou								08071280	5	
	Access 1: Camp Paradise									Fee
	Access 2: FM 2100									
	Access 3: Ponderosa Marine	•				•	•			Fee
East Fork, San Jacinto River								08070200	5	
	Lake Houston: Alexander Deussen Park	•	•		•		•		10	
San Jacinto River below Lake Houston								08072050		
	Eisenhower Park	•	•		•		•		11	
	Rio Villa Park		•				•			
Cypress Creek										
	Access 1: Meyer Park						•	08068900	4	
	Access 2: Kuykendahl Road crossing						•		8	
	Access 3: Mercer Arboretum	•	•		•		•	08069000	6	Call in advance to use access
Spring Creek								08068275		Upstream gage
	Access 1: Old Riley Fuzzell Road Crossing							08068500	2.8	
	Access 2: Pundt Park	•	•		•	•	•	08060500	8.3	Call in advance to use access; desirable gage level 1.5 to 10 feet
	Access 3: Jesse Jones Park and Nature Center	•	•		•		•		4	Call in advance to use access
	Access 4: Edgewater Park						•			
Lake Woodlands		•	•			•	•		5	Northshore Park; daylight
Greens Bayou							•	08076000	4	
Buffalo Bayou							•	08072700		Mayde Creek gage
	Access 1: TX 6 crossing						•	08073500	1.5	
	Access 2: Terry Hershey Park at Memorial Mews		•		•		•		5	
	Access 3: Terry Hershey Park at Wilcrest				•				6	
	Access 4: Briar Bend Park		•				•	08073700	6	
	Access 5: Woodway Crossing								8	
	Access 6: Hogg Bird Sanctuary						•			
	Access 7: Eleanor Tinsley Park		•				•		0.25	
	Acess 8: Sabine Street canoe launch						•		0.5	
	Acess 9: Allen's Landing, Park/Main Street						•	08074000	4	Parking fee
Brays Bayou								08074840		
	Segment 1: Art Storey Park	•			•		•		3.5	Take-out at Braeburn Glen Park
	Segment 2: MacGregor Park to Mason Park						•		5	
Sims Bayou								08075500		
	Reveille Park						•		7	
	Milby Park		•				•			
Vince Bayou								08075730	1.5	
Sheldon Reservoir		•	•	•		•	•		5	Sheldon Lake State Park
Carpenters Bayou							•			Sheldon Lake State Park

5 San Jacinto–Brazos Coastal Basin

BETWEEN THE MOUTH of the San Jacinto River on Galveston Bay west to where the Brazos River flows into the Gulf of Mexico are a large number of water bodies that empty directly into Galveston Bay, and thence into the Gulf of Mexico. These form the San Jacinto–Brazos Coastal Basin.

Clear Creek and Clear Lake

Clear Creek forms the southern boundary of Harris County, and northern boundary for Galveston and Brazoria counties. It rises in Fort Bend County and runs for 41 miles through Clear Lake and into Galveston Bay. Pearland, Friendswood, and League City are drained, and periodically flooded, by its waters. In the late 1990s the US Army Corps of Engineers agreed to prepare a revised plan to mitigate flooding in the area. I attended several public hearings concerning the "improvements" that would attain the desired end and am pleased that, to date at least, the concreting and straightening options seem to have been mitigated. League City is planning an eco-friendly Clear Creek Nature Park to maintain its natural character. Clear Creek Environmental Foundation looks out for the health and well-being of the creek.

We are not the first humans to live along its banks. An archaeological reconnaissance of the second reach of the Flood Control Project in 1990 found eleven sites: eight from prehistoric times and three from historic times. John Williams built a house on the banks of Clear Creek in 1824. Stock raising was the main economic basis for the area until the 1890s, at least for League City and the Butler cattle ranch. In 1895 a colony of English Quakers (Religious Society of Friends) purchased 1,500 acres from J. C. League and started the settlement of Friendswood.

The upper reaches of Clear Creek are shaded by hardwood trees that touch above the waterway. It becomes wider as it approaches League City, and by the time it reaches I-45, the creek becomes more and more marshlike in character. Large mudflats are visible from the freeway and more easterly crossings (TX 3 and FM 270) when tides are low. Shore and wading birds are seen frequently on the mudflats; upper reaches are renowned for "fallouts" of warblers and other migratory birds under the right conditions and time of year.

Access 1: Frankie Carter Randolph Park

Although I am using this as the uppermost access point, it is possible to paddle even higher up the creek. This park is on FM 2351, west and south of its crossing with Clear Creek. However, on the opposite side of 2351 is 1776 Bicentennial Park—a much more convenient place to park and move canoes down the steep banks to the creek. Randolph Park is marked on more maps but does not have a developed or convenient place to put in. Clear Creek's winding course travels at least 7 miles to make up the 4 miles as the crow flies to Countryside Park. Twice I have taken inexperienced paddlers on this stretch; they were very tired by the time we got to the end, so I don't recommend this as one of your first few trips

Access 2: Countryside Park

Both this park and Randolph Park have nice restroom facilities and paved parking. Countryside also has playing fields for soccer, a covered basketball court, and access to several miles of hiking trails. Bay Area Boulevard has been completed across Clear Creek only for a few years so may not be indicated on older maps. Countryside Park is on the south side of the

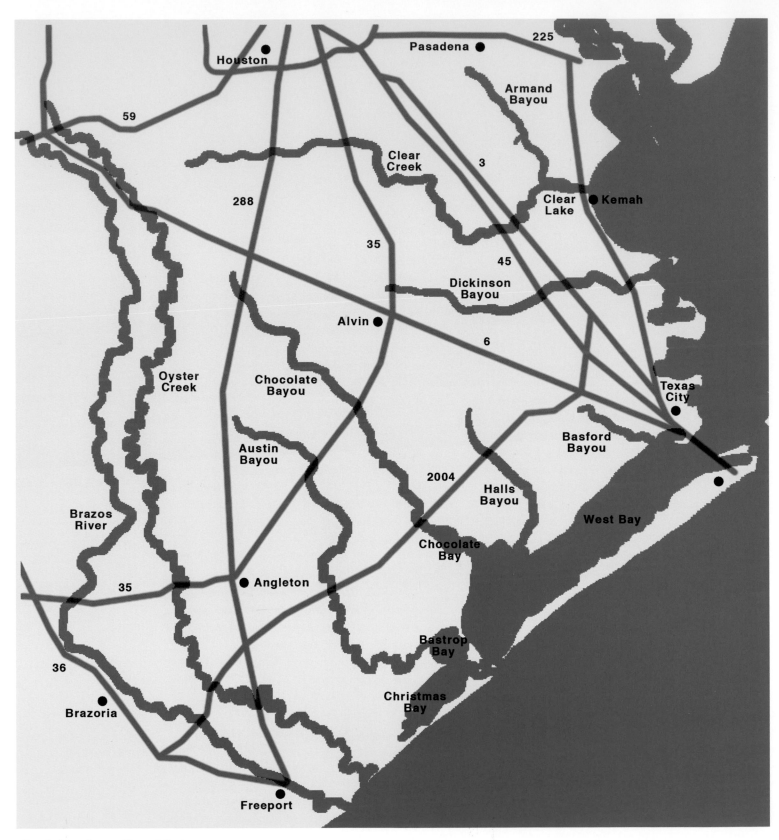

San Jacinto–Brazos Coastal Basin

Clear Creek

Upper reaches of Clear Creek, below Randolph Park

creek, east of Bay Area Boulevard, north of FM 518, and south of FM 528.

The creek is wider here, but tree lined. As you head downstream, it will get wider and marshes will appear on both sides; there are also more houses, some of which are visible from the bayou. The next stopping place downstream is only about 3 miles.

Access 3: Challenger Seven Memorial Park

The downside to the access at Challenger Seven is that use of its multiple concrete boat launches is

discouraged. If you are paddling with a group that can prove it is insured, you can get permission to take out or put in here. Otherwise, you may have to make it a brief stop for restroom facilities and head on. If you return after your paddle, you will find nice walking trails and marsh observation stations. The park has many programs for students and is managed by Harris County. Call 713-440-1587 for reservations and information.

I once ran a Girl Scout paddling trip downstream from Countryside to Challenger Seven and back upstream. I don't believe I was too popular with the girls or adults, who were a bit tired after the upstream paddle. You might avoid doing this if you want to maintain your popularity among your friends.

This stretch will be well populated with motorboats in the warm months of the year. To my surprise when I registered for the Challenger Seven stop, the park managers insisted that I have *two* sheriff deputies in motorboats accompany our group—one ahead of us and one behind. I don't know if they thought we were so inept we would turn over and drown in the creek or if they feared our being run over by motorboats. The only other time I have been accompanied by officers of the law was also on Clear Creek, but a stretch much farther upstream. On that occasion, they had to actually arrest one of the boaters who refused to slow down for us, even with our escort!

Access 4: Walter Hall Park

This park is managed by League City and is just west of TX 3 where it crosses Clear Creek. You can hardly miss its large entrance sign; drive in and find the boat ramp next to the creek. A lot of fairs and community activities are held here; you may be able to participate in landlubber activities as well as boating. The next access is about 2 miles downstream.

Access 5: FM 270 Boat Ramp

There are many embayments and much marshland along this segment. Clear Creek Nature Park opened in 2009 on the south side of the creek, just to the east of FM 270. It has restrooms and parking available as well as picnic tables and nature trails.

From here it is a long way to the next public access point. The creek twists and turns as you wind around Nassau Bay (a takeoff on "NASA," which is directly across the NASA Parkway from Nassau Bay) and emerge on Clear Lake. Clear Lake is reputed to be one of the largest marinas in the world, a safe harbor for thousands and thousands of sailboats. There are a Jet Ski rental shop here and many motorboats, so expect wind effects and lots of chop, whether or

Clear Creek pipeline, an unmistakable sign that you are getting closer to Countryside Park. Note how much wider the bayou is here.

not there is wind. I paddle this leg only in the colder months of the year because of the heavy traffic. The take-out is along the north shore at Clear Lake Park, which has both a south (on Clear Lake) and north (on Mud Lake) part. The south segment has concrete ramps and is frequented by the motoring crowd; the north part on Mud Lake houses the Bay Area Rowing Club and is also popular with the windsurfing set. It is about 6 miles from the FM 270 boat ramp to Clear Lake Park south.

Accesses 6 and 7: Clear Lake Park, North (6) and South (7)

Clear Lake Park north is a good take-out or launching site. Clear Lake Park south is on Clear Lake and has been held open 24 hours per day, but there is some talk of shutting it down late at night. I have used this as a launching site for moonlight paddles across Mud Lake (no boats with motors are supposed to be in here or north to Armand Bayou). During one particular paddle, the night sky had a supernatural pink/orange glow from refineries in the area. You can make special arrangements with the Bay Area Park for night paddles if you are willing to take responsibility for a group.

Access 8: Ben Blackledge Public Boat Ramp

This boat ramp is practically under the high Kemah/ Seabrook bridge, south of the bridge and west of TX 146. It's about 3 miles from the Clear Lake Park sites and a convenient take-out if you want to cruise Clear Lake to see all the big marinas or just want to paddle across the lake. If you take the channel under 146, you could go on up to Seabrook or take in the spectacle of Kemah Boardwalk on Galveston Bay. This water-way is *very* congested with sailboats, under power and otherwise, a high-speed tourist boat from Kemah, and even some commercial shrimp boats, so be very careful. Travel in a group and/or close to shore—make sure other boaters see you; they are not looking for a craft the size of a canoe or kayak. If your luck is of the extreme variety, maybe you can find pieces of eight, reputedly sunken treasure left behind by pirates.

Taylor Bayou and Taylor Lake

Public access to these connected water bodies is from Red Bluff Road where it crosses the lake. It is fre-quented by personal watercraft in the warmer months. As you head north, upstream, the bayou goes under TX 146 and for about a mile is a very pretty natural bayou, then becomes a channelized ditch. Downstream, the lake opens out and is ringed by houses, with a wide-open surface area that is subject to wind.

Armand Bayou Complex

Armand Bayou is one of the least disturbed bayous in the Houston area. It is protected by the Armand Bayou Nature Center's holdings as one of the largest urban wil-derness preserves in the United States. It lies mostly in the city limits of Pasadena and is designated as a Coastal Preserve. It is also a TPWD Coastal Paddling Trail. No gasoline-powered engines are permitted on the bayou, making it a premier paddling place in the Houston area.

The area was visited by Native Americans for seven thousand years. In the early to mid-nineteenth century it was known as Middle Bayou, and a small settlement of French farmers and subsistence hunters and fishers lived here for about forty years just north of where Bay Area Boulevard now crosses Armand Bayou. The settlement vanished by the turn of the century. By the early twentieth century the bayou was part of a 30,000-acre ranch owned by Jim West, who built the huge mansion you can see today looking over NASA Parkway and Clear Lake. At one time it housed the Lunar and Planetary Space Institute.

There are six sites that have direct access to the bayou and its tributaries: Armand Bayou Nature Cen-ter (fee for admission; not a good access for private boats), Bay Area Park, Clear Lake Park north, Clear Lake Park south, Armand Bayou Hike and Bike Trail boat launch, and Middlebrook Drive. Bay Area Park is where I usually access the bayou. It has a paved park-ing area, easy access to the water, and nice restroom facilities plus playgrounds for children, multiple baseball playing fields, a dog park, and picnic areas.

The main bodies of water that are part of this complex are Mud Lake, Horsepen Bayou, Big Island Slough, and Armand Bayou itself. Extensive subsidence in the 1960s and 1970s makes the bayou look more pondlike than in its earlier history. Although subsid-ence has slowed or stopped today, you can see many drowned trees still standing where there used to be dry land. Extensive planting activities of Galveston Bay Foundation and other organizations are helping to restore marshlands that disappeared with subsidence.

It is a quiet place to take a peaceful paddle and enjoy both upland hardwood forest and coastal prairies and marshes. Wildlife is protected here. There are many deer and *lots* of alligators and alligator gar (fish). I have even seen at least one huge feral hog. Wading birds are always in evidence, so expect to see great blue herons, American egrets, snowy egrets, and many others. Look for ospreys ("fish eagles"), black vultures, and a wide variety of forest birds.

Mud Lake

This is the southern terminus of Armand Bayou before it enters Clear Lake farther south. It is a popular windsurfing and rowing site, bounded to the south by NASA Parkway. Its next neighbor to the west is the

146

Red Bluff Rd

Big Island
Slough

Big Island
Slough Access

Armand
Bayou

Bay Area Blvd

Taylor
Bayou

Middlebrook Dr

Bay
Area Park

Armand Bayou
Nature Center

University of Houston
Clear Lake

Horsepen
Bayou

Kirby Dr

Mud
Lake

Taylor
Lake

Space
Center Blvd

Clear Lake
Park N

Johnson Space Center

NASA Parkway

Clear Lake
Park S

Clear Lake

N
W E
S

0   .5   1

Armand and Taylor Bayous

Johnson Space Center. The low docks provided for rowers are very nice for canoe and kayak launching, but you may want to avoid heavy-use times by the rowing teams.

Horsepen Bayou

From Bay Area Park, head south and look for the tin boat shed of Armand Bayou Nature Center to your left (east); head in the opposite direction, and you will see the entrance to Horsepen Bayou along the left bank. Coastal Preserve marker 9 is right at the entrance. Your trip to the University of Houston at Clear Lake campus is about 2 miles each way, or 4 miles round-trip. You can also get to Horsepen Bayou from Clear Lake Park, but its entrance is about 3 miles from Clear Lake Park plus another 1 or 1.5 miles. You are paddling through a bottomland hardwood forest on the bayou. It is shaded for most of its length, although getting to the bayou from Armand Bayou involves paddling through much more open water so you are susceptible to strong winds. Ospreys are almost always in this area and north of Bay Area Boulevard. Some birds are here year-round, but you will see many more during migration season. You will also see large roosts for black vultures as you approach Horsepen Bayou from Armand Bayou—they are really obvious in the winter when leaves are off the trees.

Big Island Slough

This straightened waterway makes for a 3.5-mile round-trip from Bay Area Park. From the park, head

A quiet day on Mud Lake after Hurricane Ike

under Bay Area Boulevard and hug the right bank of the stream past the first right turn several hundred yards beyond the boulevard. Although it is a dug waterway, it has naturalized to fairly mature stands of bottomland hardwoods, as well as pine trees on some of the higher areas. It is nicely protected from prevailing southeasterly winds, but be aware that you will likely have to paddle into the winds on your return to Bay Area Park. You can also access the slough from the Armand Bayou Hike and Bike Trail.

Armand Bayou Access Points

You can paddle for miles on the main body of the bayou. The best access is from Bay Area Park. Paddle upstream under Bay Area Boulevard, and you can travel for many miles before the stream becomes too small to navigate. It is tidally affected, but there is always enough water to paddle either upstream or downstream. The downstream leg, in the opposite direction from the Bay Area Boulevard bridge, will take you to Mud Lake or to the entrance of Horsepen Bayou to the west.

Access Point 1: Bay Area Park

➡ *Directions.* Armand Bayou is southeast of downtown Houston. From the Gulf Freeway (I-45), take the Bay Area Boulevard exit and head east. In about 7 miles, you will pass the University of Houston–Clear Lake entrance signs and soon cross Armand Bayou. Just past the bridge, take the second driveway to your right, which is marked "Bay Area Park." Follow the entry road (slowly!), and you will come to a large parking lot with easy access to the water. Park there, put your boat in the water, and away you go.

If you are approaching from TX 146, head west on Red Bluff Road in Seabrook. Travel about 2 to 3 miles to the traffic light intersection with Bay Area Boulevard, and turn left (west). You will pass the Armand Bayou Nature Center on your left shortly before you come to the Bay Area Park entrance.

Black vultures, a common sight at Armand Bayou

Access Point 2: Clear Lake Park North

➡ *Directions.* From the Gulf Freeway (I-45), exit at NASA Parkway and head east. In about 6 miles you will notice Clear Lake immediately south of the road. At the first traffic signal past Clear Lake, turn left into Clear Lake Park north. From TX 146, just north of the Kemah/Seabrook bridge, turn west on NASA Parkway. In 3 miles, turn right to Clear Lake Park north at the traffic signal. You will know if you have gone too far if you see the West mansion on your right and Clear Lake on your left! Your put-in from here is on Mud Lake.

Access Point 3: Clear Lake Park South

➡ *Directions.* From the Gulf Freeway (I-45), exit at NASA Parkway and head east. In about 6 miles you will notice Clear Lake immediately south of the road. Mud Lake will be on your left; when you get to the far end of Mud Lake, turn right into the parking lot. From TX 146, just north of the Kemah/Seabrook bridge, go west on NASA Parkway. In 3 miles, about one-fourth mile past the traffic signal, turn left to Clear Lake Park south, its large parking lot, and boat ramp.

Spanish moss draping a tree on the banks of Armand Bayou

This puts you at a boat launch site on Clear Lake. Its advantage is that it is open 24 hours per day; and if you want to paddle under NASA Parkway and upstream through Mud Lake to Armand Bayou for a night trip, your car won't be locked in the parking lot on your return.

Access Point 4: Armand Bayou Hike and Bike Trail Boat Launch

Where Bay Area Boulevard crosses Big Island Slough, there are parking spaces and picnic tables with direct access to Big Island Slough. You will spot wild grapes along here in season; look for wild Turk's cap hibiscus and the bright red cardinal flowers. The bayou is paddleable farther upstream, although the banks have been clear-cut and the waterway is much more exposed. While paddling here one evening, I was surprised by many deer grazing the grassy banks and saw a large cottonmouth moccasin that climbed easily over an 18-inch Styrofoam block to head on up the bank.

Access Point 5: Middlebrook Drive

Where Middlebrook Drive crosses Horsepen Bayou is an unimproved access point to the bayou. Farther upstream, University Drive and Bay Area Boulevard also cross. At University Drive, the access from University of Houston has been fenced off, presumably to keep large alligators from entering their pond at the edge of campus, but if you don't mind a long carry to the water, you can get to it there.

Note: Shoreline Publishing Company has a very nice Armand Bayou Paddling Trail Photomap available. I purchased mine at the Nature Center. It is very useful, with GPS coordinates and the placement of trail markers indicated.

Dickinson Bayou

The bayou, bay, and town take their name from John Dickinson, an early Harris County settler and member of Stephen F. Austin's "Old Three Hundred" colonists. In August 1824 he purchased a strip of land a mile wide between League City and Galveston Bay, and by 1850 there was a settlement on the bayou. In 1857 Ebenezer Nichols built a summer home by the bayou. If you look closely at the north bank of the bayou, you can see the house in its yellow glory in a stand of large trees about a half mile downstream from the railroad bridge and TX 3.

The lower part of the bayou, from I-45 to the bay, has a lot of residential housing. Above I-45 it becomes a lot wilder in nature; close to the bay it widens out into open marshland. At its midpoint you can see some really nice homes, and one in particular has an incredible variety of palm trees surrounding it. At night they are lit up and spectacular. One of the distinctive natural features of Dickinson is all the pine trees that grow in the sandy soil and numerous big trees in general for this coastal plain town. An interesting bird feature is the night rookery for hundreds of black vultures—look for them along FM 517 eastbound at dusk.

There are at least three public access points to Dickinson Bayou. Its depth and breadth make it very attractive to powerboats as well, and in the lower reaches some fair-sized commercial boats, although the TX 146 crossing limits access by sizable sailboats.

Access 1: Paul Hopkins Park

➡ *Directions.* From the Gulf Freeway (I-45), exit on FM 517 and head east. Hopkins Park is on your right (south side of 517) about three-fourths mile from the freeway and a block beyond where Maple Street enters on the left side of 517.

This is my first choice among the public places to launch. There's a nice little park here with distinctive Norwegian-style gazebos right on the water. In December the city of Dickinson puts on a festival of lights in the park, a child-friendly activity for an after-dark paddle, but be sure you have a good working

Dickinson Bayou

*View of Paul Hopkins Park
from Dickinson Bayou*

*Dickinson Bayou as it narrows
west of its pass under I-45*

flashlight in your boat for signaling approaching boats, if there are any. You can put in from TX 3 and paddle to the park. You likely will not be able to find a parking space when the festival is ongoing. Benson Bayou is the smaller bayou joining Dickinson Bayou at the park, so you can put in on it or the main bayou. When there is no festival going on, you can find parking spaces, restrooms, and a picnic area. There are plenty of trees for shade and a long stream bank for a put-in place.

■ *Paddling Note.* If you would like to see the natural bayou and possibly get away from motorcraft, head upstream and under the I-45 bridge. Be cautious under the bridge; the waterway is quite constricted here, and more than likely you will not be the only craft on the water.

Access 2: TX 3 Public Boat Ramp

This is an improved ramp, and you will see lots of motorcraft putting in here on a warm day. Many homeowners along the bayou have their own lifts and docks, but in contrast to boaters on Clear Creek, most boaters here travel at slower speeds.

Access 3: TX 146 Public Boat Ramp

This ramp is much like the ramp at TX 3. Neither has restroom facilities, but there are parking and access to the water. An interesting sidelight to paddling upstream from here, or downstream from either of the other two access points, is Gum Bayou, tucked in a little backwater about halfway between the two highway crossings. It flows under FM 517 and is a delightful, intimate (i.e., not very wide) coastal bayou with alternating pastureland and tree cover. There was extensive building going on when I paddled the bayou, so its natural state may not still exist. The day I was on it, indigo bushes were in full bloom, the nicest stand of this shrub I have seen. Dickinson Bay has a bird island created by the Beneficial Uses Group for the Houston Ship Channel, using dredge spoil to build the islands. I understand this has been very successful.

If you paddle south along the Dickinson Bay shoreline, you will reach Skyline Drive boat ramp at the entrance to Moses Lake. Wading birds are here on reefs and the shoreline.

West Coast of Galveston Bay

There are numerous access points along the western shores of Galveston Bay. The Texas General Land Office's *Texas Beach and Bay Access Guide* does a very good job of describing them. Hurricane Ike, which hammered the shoreline, arrived after the publication of the guide (which advises you to call ahead for complete directions and update to site conditions), so plan with caution. I will cover only a few selected access points that I think are particularly nice for canoes or kayaks.

Access 1: Pine Gully Park

The Pine Gully of the park name is actually a pretty little bayou with clear water. Before the City of Houston constructed the Bayport Terminal, Pine Gully had direct access to Galveston Bay, but a sandbar formed at its mouth, blocking the flow of water. You may have to carry your boat over the bar to get to the bay, but it is a nice, short exploratory paddle if you decide you don't want to go out into the open water.

Access 2: Sylvan Beach Park

This park dates from the nineteenth century when the trains used to come through La Porte with visitors from all over the United States. Now the park is owned by Harris County, and part of it is leased by the City of La Porte. It has an enormous playground, a boat ramp, and direct access to Galveston Bay.

Access 3: Texas City Dike

I do not recommend this as a place to put canoes and kayaks in the water because of its wind, wave, and current exposure. Heavy commercial shipping traffic in both the Houston Ship Channel and the Texas City Channel create unpredictable water effects. Large ships have a tremendous displacement that pushes a huge bow wave and creates both low- and high-water levels as they pass by in restricted channels. These huge ships can neither turn nor stop without running aground or losing steerage. I do not recommend crossing shipping channels. A paddling destination that may have appeal from the end of the dike is a trip around Pelican Island.

You will, however, have to cross the Gulf Intracoastal Waterway in an area heavily affected by any traffic in the Texas City Channel. I have had at least one "very interesting" experience with a 4-foot breaking wave coming my way from one of these ships, and only good luck saved me from an involuntary dump.

Access 4: TPWD Boat Ramp

➡ *Directions.* On the mainland side of the I-45 Causeway to Galveston Island is a free launching place. To get to the boat ramp, exit at Tiki Island, follow the frontage road on the west side of I-45 back north, and continue straight into the parking lot instead of taking the road going back under the causeway.

This is a popular put-in for access to the bay area west of the causeway, recommended for sea kayaks only. If you stick to the north shore of Jones Bay, you get a close-up view of marshes and wetlands; there is a cut that separates Tiki Island from the mainland, or you can get a close-up view of the many expensive homes on Tiki. Head out into Galveston Bay to observe the bird sanctuaries on North and South Deer Island (no landing on these islands).

Highland Bayou

➡ *Directions.* This is an out-and-back trip as described, heading northwest from the put-in at Mahan Park. To get to Mahan Park, take the Gulf Freeway (I-45) to Exit 10 (FM 519). From the southbound frontage road, turn right (west) at 519, but do not take the second curve to the right on 519. Proceed straight ahead to the T-intersection, where a brown park sign to Highland Bayou and Mahan Park directs you to turn left. This is Lake Road. You will go through a cut in the flood-control levee and then make the next right turn onto Woodland Road (there's a brown sign here to Mahan Park). About a quarter mile down Woodland Road, you will see Mahan Park on your left. Turn into the second of the two entrances, past the ball fields, less than a quarter-mile total distance to the gravel turnaround parking lot that you can see when you clear the ball fields. The boat ramp is at the end of the gravel turnaround.

Highland and Basford bayous

South and east of Mahan Park is Highland Bayou Park, and the bayou continues southeast to empty into Galveston Bay. This stretch has little or no wind protection along its banks (the upper stretch does), so it would be best suited to sea kayaks or paddling on a day when northerly winds, instead of the prevailing southeasterlies, are forecast. The trip is 8.5 miles round-trip from Mahan Park.

This pretty little bayou is south of Houston close to the small towns of La Marque and Hitchcock. Although parts of it have modern homes built along the banks, two cemeteries, and even a travel trailer park, it is mostly unspoiled. Large oak trees grow along the banks, and in some spots wild roses have grown out on the trees over the water and provide a beautiful display in early spring. Many birds, both aquatic and terrestrial, fly overhead in search of food, including a large purple martin colony in at least one of the backyards.

■ *Paddling Note.* Unload, and then move your vehicle so boat trailers have plenty of turnaround space from the lot. Head upstream (to your right), and you're on your way. Your paddle will take you under several road overpasses; the turnaround is about 4 miles upstream where FM 2004 crosses the bayou. This is the fourth road crossing, after Vauthier Road, 519, and Delaney Road. On the return trip, you can paddle north up a tributary that enters the bayou between 519 and Vauthier Road. FM 519 will cross this tributary, too, and just beyond it is Carbide Park, a good place to land and use restroom facilities or have a picnic lunch at tables provided right off the bayou.

One note of caution: Do not be tempted, as I was, to try to use Jack Brooks Park as a put-in for this bayou. Its nice canoe launch is in fact on Highland Bayou, but what was not obvious to me is that the "real" Highland Bayou, the natural one, disappears through two large culverts right by the launch—and what you will end up on instead is the Highland Bayou Flood Control ditch. It has a lot more water than the natural bayou but is totally "manufactured," with wind-tunnel-effect, grassy, uniformly sloped sides. It's not very aesthetic and a bear of a place to get stuck in a high wind! But you can paddle for miles if you really want a workout. This anomaly is not well marked on older maps.

Basford Bayou

There is a natural Basford Bayou and a channelized Basford Bayou that open to Jones Bay. The natural bayou is a lot more aesthetically pleasing for paddling through the marsh several miles inland. Access it from Jones Bay—it is recommended for sea kayaks only.

Halls Bayou

Halls Bayou has little encroachment of civilization on it, particularly in its upper reaches. It is accessible from the public boat ramp where FM 2004 crosses. From the ramp you can paddle more than 5 miles upstream, but you will have to return to the ramp to take out. Alternatively, you can paddle downstream to Chocolate Bayou, 10 miles away. From that bayou you would have to paddle several miles upstream to reach another boat

Looking across Basford Bayou's coastal wetlands to Texas City refineries in the distance

N
W · E
S

35

6

Chocolate Bayou
County Park

Albert Finkle
Memorial County Park

2917

Liverpool

2004

171

Chocolate
Bayou

Halls
Bayou

Boat Ramp

Chocolate
Bay

Halls
Lake

West Galveston Bay

Intracoastal
Waterway

Chocolate and Halls bayous

0   1.5   3

ramp (on Chocolate Bayou), which would be a rather vigorous paddle.

Chocolate Bayou

Chocolate Bayou is south of Houston, just outside the town of Alvin. In 1996 I would have given it a rave review for its tall trees and shaded banks, but I was very disappointed to have paddled it recently and found that most of the big trees and all of the underbrush had been cleared from the west bank of the stream for most of the length of the paddle from Chocolate Bayou to Finkle Park. Chocolate Bayou runs basically north/south, so its potential for late-afternoon summer paddles was clearly there as long as the tall trees stood and provided shade. I would not recommend that now, but it is a nice wintertime paddle, particularly with a north wind.

There is another hazard to deal with as well: a low-water dam about two-thirds into the paddle. It is clearly marked, and there is a good place to get out and line boats over the dam on river left. At high-water levels this could be a very dangerous spot. Be sure to scout before attempting to run. Scout at low levels, too—you could damage the underside of your canoe, or worse yet, think the dam is safely runnable when it isn't. Take every precaution.

Otherwise, it's still a nice paddle, with good put-in and take-out spots. A slow-paced group can run the 3.5 miles of the first stretch in 4 hours. If you decide that's just not enough for one day, you can add another 10 miles and go on to the FM 2004 high bridge, a total of 13.5 miles from Chocolate Bayou Park. If you would like to explore Chocolate Bay more fully, paddling toward the Gulf from 2004 will get you to Alligator Point in another 8 miles. From 2004 south it is quite wide open and subject to wind, tide, current, and the wakes of sizable boats, as well as oyster reef hazards. I have paddled this segment in both canoe and sea kayak—the latter is the recommended craft.

Access 1: Chocolate Bayou County Park
➜ *Directions.* Take TX 35 south from Alvin. Shortly after 35 intersects with CR 2917, it crosses Chocolate Bayou; immediately on the left past the bayou is Chocolate Bayou County Park. Turn left into the park, and follow the paved road to the boat ramp on the bayou. It appears the signage has been removed, but the park remains.

Opposite the turn to Chocolate Bayou County Park is a sign for Camp Mohawk. Formerly a private youth camp, it has been renovated as a county park with overnight camping and bunkhouse accommodations. It does not have direct bank access to Chocolate Bayou but would be a very convenient place to camp near the bayou. There are plans to offer kayaking instruction and nature study at the park; be sure to check out the Brazoria County Parks Web site for up-to-date information (www.brazoria-county.com/parks/).

From Chocolate Bayou Park, you can paddle upstream for several miles until a logjam impedes progress. The beauty of this segment is that it is still mostly wooded with a fair amount of natural vegetation in place. Whether you head upstream or downstream,

Saltwater intrusion dam on Chocolate Bayou; portage required. Photo by Marilyn Kircus

one of the unusual vegetative features is the large stands of horsetail fern that have thrived in the increased daylight after the trees were cut down; the plant can also withstand at least the periodic mowing that "enhances" the storm-drainage capacity of the stream—or at least that is how I interpret the need for clear-cutting and mowing.

When you make the downstream run from Chocolate Bayou Park, you will have several miles' paddling before you will see "WARNING" and "DANGER" signs and a string of red lights on the low-water dam. On the left bank as you are facing downstream is an old (and appears to be inoperable) boat lift (see photo of saltwater intrusion dam). The dock by the lift makes getting out of boats and moving them over the dam fairly easy, but be very careful not to get into the backwash of the water over the dam. My most recent trip downstream was very odd in this location—the waters downstream were 6 inches higher than the upstream waters! I think the dam is a saltwater barrier to keep saltier bay waters from moving upstream in periods of low stream flow. If those salty waters were to be pumped onto rice fields, the crops and fields would be ruined. The length of the run from Chocolate Bayou Park to Albert Finkle Memorial County Park is about 3.5 miles.

As you get close to Finkle Park, you can enjoy the overhanging oak trees along a natural stretch of bayou that has not been cut. It is interesting to notice how deeply the bayou has cut into the soil for most of the length of this trip.

Access 2: Albert Finkle Memorial County Park

➡ *Directions.* When you have unloaded your boats, you can run a shuttle by heading back toward Alvin on TX 35, but this time turn right on CR 2917. In about 3 miles you will intersect CR 171. Turn right on 171, and follow it to where it makes a hard left-hand turn. At that point, turn right into Albert Finkle Memorial County Park for your take-out. The park has picnic tables and a playground for kids but no restrooms (nor are there any at Chocolate Bayou Park).

Access 3: FM 2004 Boat Ramp

If you wish to have a more rigorous trip, you can add 10 miles to the length of the trip by making your alternate take-out where FM 2004 crosses Chocolate Bayou. There's a high bridge there and a large parking lot with ramps for motorboats. Expect a fair amount of fishing traffic.

If you are a sea kayaker and enjoy seeing marshland birds, put in at 2004 and paddle downstream until you are almost into the Gulf, 6 miles downstream, then left and into the marshlands. You will have a lot of wind and motor traffic exposure there, thus the sea kayak recommendation. There are also lots of oyster reefs that are invisible until you run up on them, so you may have to stick fairly close to the main boat channel until you get closer to the Gulf. A July trip was a visual feast of marshland birds, their young, and all manner of brackish-water and land crabs. Be aware that there is no shade.

Austin and Bastrop Bayous

Austin Bayou is named for Henry Austin, nephew of Stephen F Austin. Henry received a grant from his uncle for property in the area of the bayou that now bears his name. The section described here is 5 miles in length before it joins Bastrop Bayou on its journey to Bastrop Bay and the Gulf of Mexico.

Felipe Enrique Neri, originally from Holland, preferred to be called the Baron de Bastrop and was a friend of Moses Austin. He became land commissioner for Stephen F. Austin, and it was he who issued 297 titles to the "Old Three Hundred" of the Austin Colony. Bastrop Bayou and Bay were named for him. Both Bastrop and Austin bayous were important water highways for the Anglo nineteenth-century presence in Texas.

Both bayous have extensive freshwater wetlands in their upstream portions. After Austin Bayou joins Bastrop Bayou, Bastrop Bayou becomes increasingly brackish as it gets close to Bastrop Bay. Austin Bayou is navigable for some distance above the FM 2004

Austin and Bastrop bayous and Lower Oyster Creek

ramp; Bastrop Bayou, less so, although it is a broad and deep bayou to the south and east.

From some maps it appears Big Slough has potential for paddling; more detailed boating maps make it appear disconnected, with no mouth on the ICW. If you paddle it and find otherwise, let me know! From the Big Slough Recreation Area you can make the 7.5-mile Big Slough drive and check it out. This is downstream of the TX 227 crossing that is the take-out for both access points described.

Access 1: Bastrop Bayou at FM 2004

There is a large paved parking lot and boat ramp here, as well as a fishing pier that is accessible to people with disabilities. Trash cans are the only additional facility. Upstream and downstream you can see homes along the bayou. From here it is 8 miles downstream to the 227 crossing and public boat ramp. At about 6.5 miles Austin Bayou joins Bastrop Bayou. This is a broad bayou through coastal prairie. It is very prone to wind effects so is probably best navigated from a sea kayak or a motorized craft, especially if the prevailing southerly winds are blowing.

Access 2: Austin Bayou at FM 2004

This segment of stream is much narrower than Bastrop Bayou, which it joins 5 miles south of 2004. It is a favorite of sea kayakers, a recommended craft because of the wind exposure. Those of us who have paddled it have always done so in the winter when we are more likely to have a tailwind from the north, the mosquitoes won't be singing as loud, and the lack of shade is not a problem. Actually, getting out of one's boat can be a challenge for lack of places that are both clear and high enough. There is one such beach close to the confluence with Bastrop Bayou. When I paddled this stretch in 2001, there was an upside-down boat at a strategic location that made a great place to scramble onto for a private picnic. It is likely not there anymore after several tropical events have passed through. Beautiful tall palmettos grow along the bayou, taller river cane, and all kinds of freshwater marsh grass, giving way to brackish-water plants farther along Bastrop Bayou.

It is 6.5 miles from the 2004 crossing to the take-out on Bastrop Bayou where CR 227 crosses.

Access 3: CR 227 Crossing of Bastrop Bayou ("Demi-John" Ramp)

This is the take-out spot for both access points 1 and 2. It has modest appeal as a put-in for a long paddle downstream, through Cox Lake, Lost Lake, across Bastrop Bay, through Cold Pass, and take-out at San Luis Park. My mapping tool records the distance as 17.5 miles. One would want to be in shape, assured of a tailwind (or a mild headwind), and in a fast and efficient boat to take on that leg! This goes right through Brazoria National Wildlife Refuge, so it is sure to be pristine and no doubt loaded with alligators and all manner of shore and wading birds. While you are in the vicinity, you can stop by the Brazoria National Wildlife Refuge Information and Discovery Center headquarters, walk the nature trail that parallels CR 227 on an abandoned railroad right-of-way, or drive the Big Slough auto route. The information and discovery complex is 3 miles down the entrance road from 227, south and west of its crossing with Bastrop Bayou. It is also one of the "birdiest" spots in Texas. Boardwalks and trails make exploration and observation easy and convenient.

Oyster Creek

The *Handbook of Texas* states, "Some believe that in 1528 Álvar Núñez Cabeza de Vaca was blown ashore at the mouth of Oyster Creek. At that time, and until they were driven out by Anglo and Tejano settlers in the 1820s, Karankawa Indians inhabited the banks of the stream." Its fertile soils were attractive to members of Stephen F. Austin's "Old Three Hundred" families, who set up farms and plantations and ran small boats on the creek to obtain supplies as well as move their goods to market. Cotton was a major crop until a wet season in 1840 ruined much of that crop, so sugarcane was planted in increasing amounts. By the peak of the sugarcane harvest before the Civil War, Brazoria County, including the plantations along

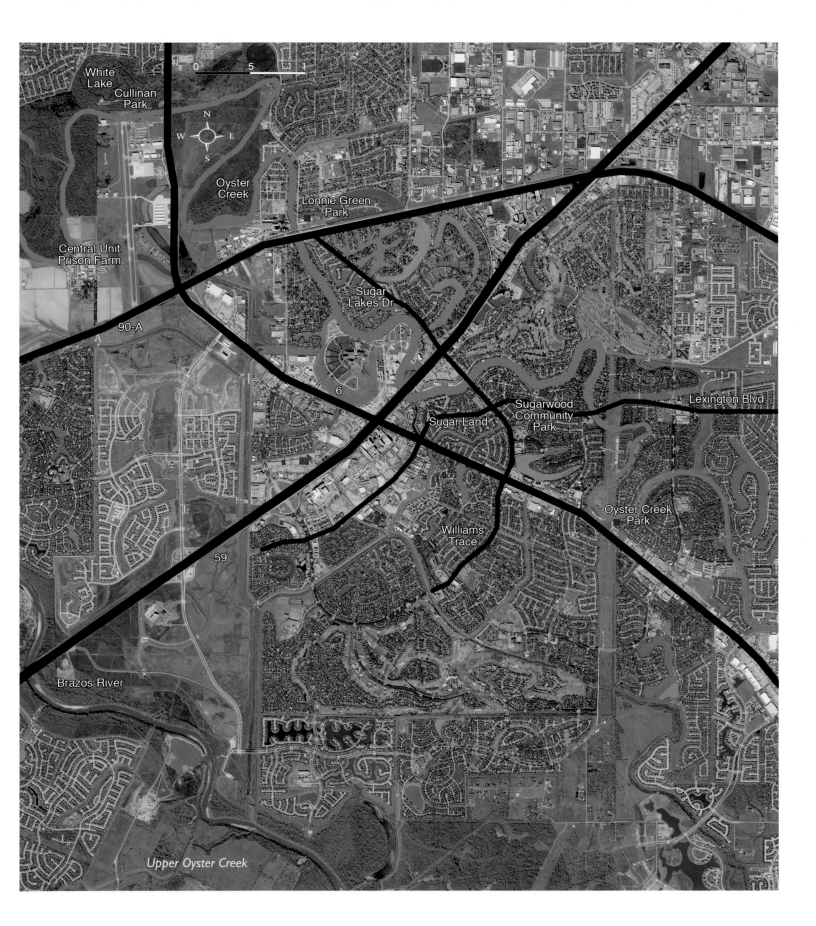

White
Lake

Cullinan
Park

Oyster
Creek

Lonnie Green
Park

Central Unit
Prison Farm

90-A

Sugar
Lakes Dr

6

Sugar Land

Sugarwood
Community
Park

Lexington Blvd

Williams
Trace

Oyster Creek
Park

59

Brazos River

Upper Oyster Creek

N
W — E
S

0   .5   1

Oyster Creek, the Brazos River, and Jones Creek, produced 75 percent of the Texas harvest.

Cane and cotton production required a large labor force, chiefly supplied by the institution of slavery before the Civil War. With the abolition of slavery, the next source of labor was prisoners who were leased to landowners. In 1882 twelve of the eighteen Texas sugar plantations utilized the labor of more than one-third of the state's prison inmates.

An interesting sociological feature of Oyster Creek is that it flows through or drains five prison farms: the former Central Unit (ceased operation as a prison farm in 2011), the Darrington Unit, Jester Units, the Ramsey Unit, and the Wayne Scott Unit, originally known as Retrieve. I will never forget my first trip on a segment near Sugar Land. The creek had narrowed to only about 20 feet across, and I was admiring the nice open farmland, the mat of water hyacinth, and large population of nutria when I spotted a tractor mired in the mud only a short distance from the water. The uniforms of the men trying to extract the tractor made me realize in short order that it was in fact a prison work team. Thankfully, they and their guard were more interested in the tractor than in two kayakers, but I suspect we should not have been there at all. There were (and are) no warning signs posted, perhaps an oversight of the prison in not expecting visitors via water.

Oyster Creek is 52 miles in length, which seems to me to be a short estimate. The stream meanders along its entire course, and as the crow flies, it is at least 50 miles from Sugar Land to the coast. The upper stretches at and above the Central Unit prison farm are about the limit of navigation for canoes and kayaks; and I would suggest paddling downstream from the first access point at Cullinan Park. Its lower reaches are tidally affected.

Middle sections of the creek flow through the Columbia bottomland, a forested area characterized by hardwood trees dominated by live oaks. The entire Columbia bottomlands region goes across all the major river drainages from at least the Brazos and Colorado rivers and extends 60 miles inland. The area is important to migratory birds and is being preserved in a project known as Austin's Woods, or the Texas Mid-Coast National Wildlife Refuge. Reports from at least two sources tell me the upper and lower parts of Oyster Creek are paddleable; the middle sections frequently have too little water—and too many prison farms—to make them a reliable or safe choice for paddling.

Access 1: Cullinan Park

Cullinan Park, owned by the City of Houston, is on TX 6, just north of its intersection with US 90A on the west side of the road. The entrance is well marked. There is no parking next to the put-in spot—look for the put-in by the creek as you enter the park, and you will see the dirt road that leads to it. Fishers have used this spot for some time, so you may be able (and allowed) to drive your vehicle close to the stream to offload your boat and equipment, but please move the vehicle to a paved parking area before you shove off.

If you are not paddling on the creek, you can enjoy White Lake inside the park from its boardwalk, pier, and observation tower. There is no boat access to this shallow lake. Picnic tables and portable toilets make visiting a more enjoyable experience.

A recent attempt at paddling Oyster Creek was aborted due to water hyacinth so thick it was impenetrable. If you see it the whole way across the bayou, you should leave your boats on their carriers and find another place to paddle. However, if there is no obstruction, paddling upstream on Oyster Creek will get you to wide, open fields next to the creek. This area was formerly the Central Unit prison farm. The City of Sugar Land has acquired the property and is in the process of developing it. Prior to 2009, getting to this stretch was no problem; in March 2009 the passageway was totally choked off by water hyacinths within one-fourth mile of the put-in both upstream and downstream.

Paddling downstream, if you can get there, may require a portage around a low bridge, but beyond that the stream will open up and increase dramatically in volume. Lonnie Green Playground is 3 miles from Cullinan Park and up a tributary to your left. You can scramble up the banks to a small park or turn around and paddle the 3 miles back to Cullinan Park for a 6-mile round-trip.

Access 2: Lonnie Green Playground

Lonnie Green Playground is located at 130 1st Street in Sugar Land. Oyster Creek's path from Cullinan Park describes a large S plus one more bend. Cleveland Lake is your left turn from Oyster Creek after you paddle past the Harmon Street bridge. There are a multitude of oxbow lakes (including Cleveland) that you can explore from this park; or you can paddle 3 miles downstream to Sugarwood Community Park. Many nice homes back up to the creek all along this length. It is about 3 miles downstream to Sugarwood Community Park.

Heading downstream (left from Cleveland Lake's entrance on Oyster Creek), you will pass under the US 90 bridge and enter a long straight stretch whose end point is a dam, which you must portage and then put in again on the downstream side. Next are the Creekbend bridge, the US 59 bridge, and then Williams Trace Boulevard.

Access 3: Sugarwood Community Park

➡ *Directions.* Sugarwood Community Park will be on your right about a mile past the Williams Trace bridge. This is not a formal access point, but a place you can park and carry boats to the water. Look for benches and tennis courts. From the intersection of Lexington Boulevard and TX 6, travel east on Lexington Boulevard to Colony Park; turn left (north) on Colony Park, and you should find yourself on a street that dead-ends by the tennis courts.

From here it is about a 3-mile paddle to the Oyster Creek Park complex; a hike-and-bike trail follows the creek for the lower part of the stretch, and you can use Lost Creek Park (3703 Lost Creek Boulevard) as an alternate take-out for a shorter paddle.

Access 4: Oyster Creek Park

This popular park is at 4033 TX 6. There are restrooms and picnic facilities at Oyster Creek Park,

which is the southern terminus on the upper paddleable section of Oyster Creek. The creek is narrow and somewhat overgrown at the park.

Access 5: Independence Park

Although not technically a part of Oyster Creek, this 46-acre lake in Independence Park, located at 2621 ½ Court Road in Missouri City, opened in 2000. Only electric motorboats or paddle-powered boats are allowed on the lake. This point is not shown on the map of Lower Oyster Creek.

Nonaccess Point: Kitty Hollow Park

Another tempting-looking small lake in the Oyster Creek area is Kitty Hollow Park, 9555 TX 6 South in Missouri City. Unfortunately, it is clearly marked "No Boating, No Canoeing, No Kayaking."

Lower Oyster Creek

From Oyster Creek Park in Sugar Land, we now jump about 60 land miles south to the second set of access points, including a second Oyster Creek Park, in the village of Oyster Creek, on the creek named Oyster Creek.

Family outing on the upper stretches of Oyster Creek. Photo by Marilyn Kircus

Access 1: Brazosport College

There is a cleared access point next to the Fine Arts Building on the east side of campus from the main entrance. Enjoy this beautifully landscaped campus. Its Natural History Museum is well worth a visit for its fine collection of shells, waterfowl, and even dinosaur bones. There is no entrance fee. While you are playing tourist in Lake Jackson, be sure to also find Sea Center Texas. The aquaria are filled with Texas and Gulf Coast native fish and wildlife, and there are nice nature walks, too. Call in advance for tours of the hatchery (979-292-0100).

You can paddle 6 miles downstream from the Brazosport campus to the next access point at Stratton Ridge boat ramp.

Access 2: Stratton Ridge Boat Ramp

→ *Directions.* This is a county-maintained ramp on CR 226, whose name in downtown Clute is Stratton Ridge Road. From TX 288 Business in Clute, travel east on Stratton Ridge Road approximately 2 miles; pass the Stratton Ridge athletic facility, and look for the ramps close to where the road crosses Oyster Creek.

From here you can paddle upstream. Oyster Creek makes a very large bend about 5 miles upstream; for the distance of paddling you will be 2 miles as the crow flies from the boat ramp. It is beautifully forested both north and south of the ramp.

Paddling downstream from the boat ramp is about a 6-mile trip to Oyster Creek Municipal Park, where FM 523 crosses Oyster Creek (the body of water) in Oyster Creek (the town). The creek is broad, and most of its length south of CR 226 is forested with large stands of live oaks. A few miles south of the boat ramp, a levee follows the banks on the west side for the rest of the distance. The day I paddled this stretch, there was no traffic at all on the levee road, and I was curious about its absence. We determined to drive the levee road back from the take-out and quickly discovered why—the road is gated and padlocked at both ends!

This is a truly beautiful stretch with few homes, just miles of oak forest or grassy slopes of the levee.

No motor traffic passed us, although clearly the creek would have been deep enough for other boats, and a few boat docks lower down implied that someone surely must boat here occasionally. Little blue herons were abundant, as well as a wide variety of birds in the trees. It took three of us paddlers in canoes about 4 hours to do this stretch. The open nature of the stream would make it vulnerable to high winds, and especially those prevailing southerlies in the summer. The shaded banks make this appealing any time of year, so long as the winds are low.

Access 3: Oyster Creek Municipal Park

→ *Directions.* If you are running a shuttle to here from the Stratton Ridge boat ramp, continue north and east on CR 226 to its intersection with FM 523. Turn right (south) on 523. After CR 792 intersects 523, look for the bridge over the creek and turn left to the boat ramp just past the bridge. The boat dock is on the east side of 523, north side of the creek; the main park (and its big sign) with a T-dock on the west side of 523 offers easy access to the banks, although a longer carry to the paved parking lot.

If you use this put-in, it is about 4 miles downstream to a point where a large loop of Oyster Creek is pinched off to form Cone Island to your west.

Access 4: CR 891 Boat Ramp

→ *Directions.* The ramp description I have shows only "CR 891 Boat Ramp." What is not clear is where the actual ramp is. The general directions are to take CR 690 north from its intersection with TX 332 just north of Surfside, and then make the first right turn (east) onto CR 891. In a very short distance you will see water both to the left and right of the road—you have just bisected the bend in the creek that defines Cone Island.

CR 891 also continues to the east almost 1.5 miles to the end of the island, where the creek has now formed a shortcut and more direct route to the ICW. There may or may not be a ramp and water access at the far end of 891. You could just paddle the 3-mile loop around Cone Island and return to the same spot

Oyster Creek between Stratton Ridge boat ramp and Oyster Creek Municipal Park

where you put in. Another alternative is to paddle south from the easternmost extremity into the ICW. On the day I was checking out the put-in/take-out, I was unable to turn on CR 891 at all; it was closed to all traffic because of pipeline construction. From Oyster Creek's mouth on the ICW it is about a mile to the Swan Lake boat ramp. To the west are other ramps (Bridge Harbor, Bridge Bait Boat Ramp) near the 332 bridge.

Facilities

San Jacinto–Brazos Coastal Basin

Paddling area	Access point	Toilet	Picnic	Camping	Water	Ramp	Parking	Gage	Mileage	Comments
Clear Creek and Clear Lake								08077540		
	Access 1: Frankie Carter Randolph Park	•	•					08077600	10	Friendswood gage
	Access 2: Countryside Park	•	•		•		•		2	
	Access 3: Challenger Seven Memorial Park	•	•		•		•		2	Must have permission in advance
	Access 4: Walter Hall Park	•	•			•	•		4	
	Access 5: FM 270 boat ramp					•	•		2	
	Accesses 6 and 7: Clear Lake Park north (6) and south (7)	•	•		•	•	•		5	
	Access 8: Ben Blackledge public boat ramp					•	•		4	
Taylor Bayou and Taylor Lake						•			4	
Armand Bayou Complex										
	Mud Lake									Southern terminus of Armand Bayou
	Horsepen Bayou									Access from Bay Area Park
	Big Island Slough								2	Access from Bay Area Park
Armand Bayou Access Points										
	Access 1: Bay Area Park	•	•		•		•		8	On Armand Bayou
	Access 2: Clear Lake Park north	•	•		•		•		2	On Mud Lake
	Access 3: Clear Lake Park south					•	•			On Clear Lake
	Access 4: Armand Bayou Hike and Bike Trail		•				•		2	On Big Island Slough
	Access 5: Middlebrook Drive								2	On Horsepen Bayou
Dickinson Bayou										
	Access 1: Paul Hopkins Park	•	•				•		5	
	Access 2: TX3 public boat ramp					•	•		1	
	Access3: TX 146 public boat ramp					•	•		3	
West Coast of Galveston Bay									20	
	Access 1: Pine Gully Park						•		2	Fee
	Access 2: Sylvan Beach Park	•	•		•		•			
	Access 3: Texas City Dike					•	•			
	TPWD boat ramp					•	•			Bait camp
Highland Bayou			•				•		4	Mahan Park or Highland Bayou Park
Basford Bayou						•	•		5	TPWD ramp access by Tiki Island
Halls Bayou						•	•		15	FM 2004 boat ramp
Chocolate Bayou										
	Access 1: Chocolate Bayou County Park					•	•	08078000	3.5	Ramp and park in poor repair
	Access 2: Albert Finkle Memorial County Park						•		7	
	Access 3: FM 2004 boat ramp					•	•		10	
Bastrop and Austin Bayous										
	Access 1: Bastrop Bayou at FM 2004								8	
	Access 2: Austin Bayou at FM 2004								6	
	Access 3: CR 227 crossing of Bastrop Bayou ("Demi-John" ramp)					•	•		17.5	
Oyster Creek										
	Access 1: Cullinan Park						•		5	
	Access 2: Lonnie Green Playground								3	
	Access 3: Sugarwood Community Park								3	
	Access 4: Oyster Creek Park								2	
	Access 5: Independence Park									
Lower Oyster Creek										
	Access 1: Brazosport College						•		9	
	Access 2: Stratton Ridge boat ramp					•	•		6	
	Access 3: Oyster Creek Municipal Park	•	•		•	•	•		4	
	Access 4: CR 891 boat ramp					•	•		6	

6 West Bay and Galveston Island

GALVESTON BAY is the largest water feature in proximity to Houston. Its water surface covers 600 square miles with an average depth of 6 to 12 feet. It supports a wide variety of uses, from commercial shipping and fishing, to water supply for home and industry, to recreational boating and the aesthetics of a water view. The bay is an estuarine system, meaning it is a coastal, semi-enclosed body of water within which saltwater from the Gulf of Mexico mixes with freshwater from the land.

There is evidence of inhabitants on Galveston Island as early as 500 BCE. By the time of Cabeza de Vaca, Karankawa peoples were on the island and to its west. The infamous pirate Jean Lafitte visited in the early nineteenth century. The hurricane here in 1900 is the greatest natural disaster to have occurred in the United States. At that time, Galveston was the largest and most prosperous city in Texas. The subsequent construction of the seawall has protected the island behind it for 10 miles of the island's 30-mile length.

Thanks to the Texas Open Beaches Act, all the beaches to the vegetation line are owned by the state, so if you can get to the beach by a public road or path, you have many miles to choose from for picnicking, fishing, or launching a boat. There are numerous places where you can get to the beach, at least on the Gulf of Mexico side of the island. Consult the Texas General Land Office's *Texas Beach and Bay Access Guide* as the most complete listing of these access points and a description of the facilities at each. I will discuss only a few of these sites. The map here of West Galveston Bay was produced prior to 2008.

Wind, waves, currents, and tides all have their effect on boating activities around the bay. The most up-to-date and accurate recording of wind, current, and tides along the Houston Ship Channel is through the Physical Oceanographic Real-Time System (PORTS) operated by the National Oceanic and Atmospheric Administration (NOAA) Center for Operational Oceanographic Products and Services. Frequent error in predictive models for water levels prompted this service. Graphing products for predicted versus observed conditions is very interesting for that aspect alone; you can find a map of the locations of the readings and the readings themselves at http://tidesandcurrents.noaa.gov/ports.

Many other sites have online tide predictions and weather forecasts. There's nothing like a trip on the open water to realize how much at the mercy of the elements you are. Take every precaution.

As you are launching a boat into the surf on the Gulf side of Galveston Island, be aware that there is a coastwise current that runs from northeast to southwest; if you are going from point to point along the beach, it is a lot easier to follow the general direction of the current. When conditions include a southerly breeze, if you tip your boat and go for an involuntary swim, you will be blown back in the general direction of the island and its beaches. If you are putting a boat in the water with a norther blowing in, your next stop for an involuntary swim may be Mexico, and it is a *long* way!

There is almost always a breeze or wind here on the coast. Sometimes the surf zone is practically flat, or it can sport some really big waves—you might want to check Galveston Island surf cameras to get an idea before you head in this direction. Some access points that are particularly nice are along the seawall (particularly the east end), in the Pocket Parks, and at Galveston Island State Park. I recommend areas without a lot of swimmers unless you have superb boat-handling skills; even if you do, it is hard to maneuver around the swimmers when the waves are running and the wind is blowing, and someone can get hurt.

The map labels, reading across the image:

0   2.5   5

30

Chocolate Bayou

Chocolate Bay

Brazoria NWR

Intracoastal Waterway

Bastrop Bay

West Galveston Bay

Jan

Sea Isle

Christmas Bay

Bay Harbor   20

29   28   27   26   22-25   21   19   18   Indian Beach   17

Bluewater Hwy / Hwy 257   San Luis Pass   Gulf of Mexico

West Galveston Bay

Galveston Island State Park

One "must-paddle" place on the island is Galveston Island State Park, on the bay side. Three paddling trails have been established there, as official State of Texas Coastal Paddling Trails. The map is a small-scale trail guide; you can buy a larger and more-detailed copy at the state park or download and print your own from the Web (www.tpwd.state.tx.us/fishboat/boat/pad-dlingtrails/coastal/galveston/). The three trails with one-way mileage given are Dana Cove (2.6 miles), Oak Bayou (4.8 miles), and Jenkins Bayou (2.8 miles). Restored coastal marshes are the main attraction. TPWD set up many paddle trails across Texas. Others in our area are at Armand Bayou, Buffalo Bayou, and the Christmas Bay Paddling Trail off the west end of Galveston Island across San Luis Pass (discussed later).

Pelican Island

I would be remiss in talking about the Galveston area if I didn't include Pelican Island, where I have been working for thirty years for Texas A&M University at Galveston (TAMUG). My personal favorite bay paddle is from right here on campus, certainly a privilege of employment, but you can do this if you call in advance and get permission from the University Police Department (409-740-4545). There are security risks associated with the US Maritime Administration training ship at the TAMUG dock and numerous boats used for research and education, so the dock is not freely available to the general public for boat launching. You can also pay the admission fee to Seawolf Park at the end of the road and launch there over the riprap; or there is a public access area on the Galveston Island side of the

Galveston Bay

Houston Ship Channel

Texas City Dike

Hwy 6

45

1

Tiki Island

2

N Deer Island

45
Galveston Causeway

Pelican Island

S Deer Island

3

Seawolf Park

9

Texas A&M

Offatts Bayou

Galveston Channel

13A
Pirates Beach

7

East End Lagoon

on Is Park

UTMB

14   13   12   11   10   8   Galveston

5   4   Stewart Beach

Seawall Blvd / Hwy 3005   6 (10,19,29,35,37,39,53,57,61st)

Pelican Island Causeway, between the sewage treatment plant and 51st Street, off old Harborside Drive.

An evening paddle from campus to the north tip of Pelican Island where the ICW cuts through is very relaxing. A colonial birds' nesting site is on that tip of the island; the small island north of the ICW is a totally protected rookery, so you should not get out of your boat there. In the right seasons you will see hundreds of birds, particularly brown pelicans and laughing gulls, on that part of the island. This is a route most suitable for sea kayaks because of the exposure to wind, weather, and tides. If you would like to make the 9-mile circular paddle around Pelican Island, you will also be paddling next to the Houston Ship Channel, by Seawolf Park, and down the Galveston Channel. I have done the paddle in less than 3 hours, but you should allow at least 4 hours

On the trail at Galveston Island State Park

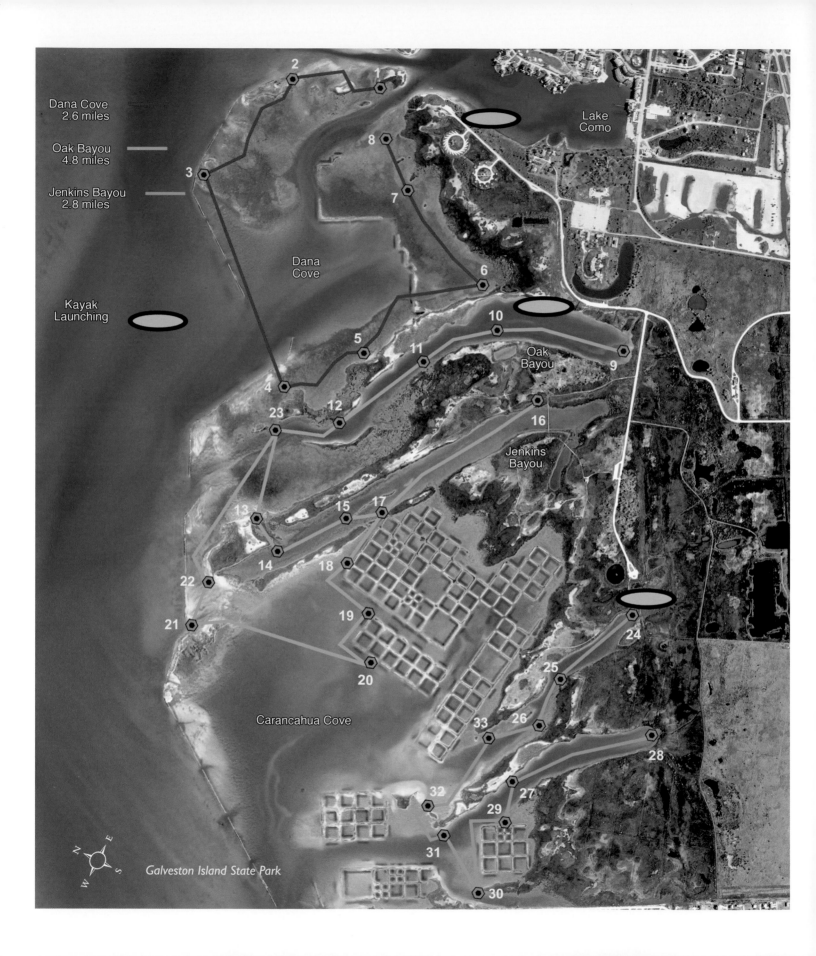

Dana Cove
2.6 miles

Oak Bayou
4.8 miles

Jenkins Bayou
2.8 miles

Kayak
Launching

Dana
Cove

Lake
Como

Oak
Bayou

Jenkins
Bayou

Carancahua Cove

Galveston Island State Park

N
E
S
W

for a more leisurely pace. If there are cruise ships or naval ships in port, you must maintain a distance of at least 400 yards.

West Galveston Bay

The north shore of West Galveston Bay has far fewer access points than the south shore of Galveston Island. The Texas Parks and Wildlife public boat ramp next to I-45 by the Tiki Island exit is one location; or you can start from the lower end of Highland Bayou where TX 6 crosses it at Louis' Bait Camp. From either you can head west through Jones Bay and pick up the ICW or use the open bay waters. I have paddled from Louis' through the ICW to Chocolate Bayou as an overnight trip, camping on a spoil island en route. Even with the worst mosquito scourge I have ever encountered on a local camping trip, it was a beautiful paddle over a Thanksgiving holiday, complete with a ringside seat to a multitude of shorebirds working the sandy shore. A shorter out-and-back trip to Greens Lake is quite nice, although a hard paddle for a one-day sea kayak trip. The new beach-house development at Harbor Walk will add a lot more human presence to what had been a wild and natural coastline; maybe you know people who live there and will let you paddle from their bulkheaded beachfront.

The next access west on the bay is at Chocolate Bayou, which is several miles' paddle upstream from the bay or 20-plus miles from the Galveston causeway.

The pelicans and cormorants of Pelican Island. Photo by Marilyn Kircus

Christmas Bay

On the far western region of the Galveston Bay system is Christmas Bay. Brazoria County's San Luis Pass Park gives good access to Christmas Bay and has campsites, showers, and restrooms available. It is a favorite paddling/fishing area for the Paddling Anglers in Canoes and Kayaks (PACK) club from Houston. Christmas Bay is one of the least disturbed areas of the entire Bay system, and as a designated Coastal Preserve, it should remain in its natural state. It consists of 4,173 acres, or 5,700 acres to the mean high-tide line boundary. To its west another 42,000 acres of Brazoria National Wildlife Refuge helps preserve its natural character and high water quality. To further enhance its natural beauty, there are 19 miles of marked Texas Coastal Paddling Trails to enjoy. The natural seagrass here supports good fishing, and Christmas Bay is a favorite destination for kayak fishers. Its variety of birdlife makes this outstanding for birders as well. There are at least two good access points to Christmas Bay: from Ernie's Too Bait Camp or from the San Luis Pass County Park. If 19 miles is a bit much for your paddling skills and condition, there are shorter 3.8- and 9-mile loops that are enjoyable and give you a good look at the bay waters.

The map for Christmas Bay shown here, like the one for Galveston Island State Park, can be downloaded from the Web (www.tpwd.state.tx.us/fishboat/boat/paddlingtrails/coastal/christmas_bay/) or purchased from Shoreline Publishing or its retailers (call 713-973-1627 for information). The map shown in the Galveston Island State Park section is a very small-scale reproduction of the paddling trails' official map—I encourage

Coastal marsh at Jones Bay

Christmas Bay

Gulf Intracoastal Waterway

you to find the original, larger map to help navigate this beautiful coastal wetlands and natural area.

The Gulf Intracoastal Waterway runs for 120 miles along the coast in the area covered by this book, from mile marker 320 on the eastern end to marker 440 before the lock at the Colorado River. It has interconnections with many other waterways. The ICW is maintained at a minimum depth of 12 feet to accommodate barge traffic and is heavily used.

When you consider that two-barge tows can carry as many as eighty rail cars or three hundred trucks, you know they are helping both traffic and air quality around our fair city. You might consider the "three hundred trucks" figure as one of these tows, and some even larger, chug down the channel that you are sharing with them. Imagine how long it would take one to stop. Their operators may not be looking out for craft as small as ours; be alert and stay out of their way.

Another interesting phenomenon of sharing the channel with barges is how much water they displace—first as water is pushed in front of them, and then the rush of water sucked back into the channel as the barge passes. You will notice the approach of a barge, even from as far away as a quarter mile. This can be quite pronounced in narrow channels, and imagine the impact of two passing in opposite directions. I have nearly

Tandem kayakers enjoying a close-up view of brown pelicans in Christmas Bay. Photo by Marilyn Kircus

been swamped more than once by this action. Barges are also very quiet for their size and run with few lights at night. Be careful out there!

There are excellent cruising guides available for the ICW—I recommend purchasing one for a detailed description of the waterways and the amenities along the route. You can go as far east as Florida and as far south as Brownsville on the Gulf ICW. Some GPS systems come preloaded with charts and maps.

Facilities

West Bay and Galveston Island

Paddling area	Access point	Toilet	Picnic	Camping	Water	Ramp	Parking	Gage	Mileage	Comments
Galveston Island State Park		●	●	●	●		●		10	State park fees and regulations apply
Pelican Island									12	
West Galveston Bay									25	
Christmas Bay									19	
Gulf Intracoastal Waterway									120	

Note:
There are many access points to the Gulf of Mexico from the Galveston Seawall and along the island at its Pocket Parks. The map on pages 120 and 121 indicates the more user-friendly access points from the seawall by the intersecting streets, listed in parentheses: 10th, 19th, 29th, 35th, 37th, 39th, 53rd, 57th, and 61st Streets. The other numbers along the Gulf side of the island indicate the Pocket Parks that have easier access points. Those range from Pocket Park 4 on the East end to Pocket Park 26 at the San Luis Pass.

Avocets on a dredge spoil island. Photo by Marilyn Kircus

7 Brazos River Basin

THE BRAZOS RIVER has been around for a very long time. Along its course are remains of some of the very first creatures and plants to live in the Paleozoic era, 540 to 250 million years ago when this area of Texas lay under shallow seas. In later eras dinosaurs wandered the area, leaving their footprints in rocks now exposed far upstream. Along the stretches described here you can find fossil shells, remains of ancient critters including dinosaurs, and petrified wood.

Los Brazos de Dios (the arms of God) is the name Coronado's expedition of 1540–42 gave to the river; one of the legends of its naming is that it saved the expedition from dying of thirst. It was not until some three hundred years later that Anglos settled by the river in appreciable numbers. Earlier Spanish settlements were attacked by hostile Native Americans, mainly Comanches, who had made living in this part of Texas so dangerous and inhospitable that earlier European attempts at settlement had failed and the area was abandoned. The first successful Anglo settlements by the river began after Moses Austin petitioned the Spanish governor in San Antonio to allow him to bring in three hundred settlers. The governor realized that having more Anglos would at least help solve the decreasing population and hostile attacks problem and granted this right to Austin. Austin died before the settlements could take place, and his son Stephen chose the location for these first settlers. The Austin Colony was established with San Felipe as its capital, on the banks of the Brazos where the Atascocita Road crossed it, near where I-10 now crosses. The colony thrived and swelled to a population of six hundred by 1836 but was burned to the ground and abandoned as the Mexican army advanced on it after the Battle of the Alamo. As you drive across this area from Houston, you will notice stands of big beautiful live oaks and large open fields that supported cotton and sugar plantations through the Civil War.

The Brazos was a transportation route for agricultural goods, chiefly cotton, sugar, and beef. It supported at least ten plantation docks, as described in Keith Guthrie's *Texas Forgotten Ports*. Steamboats plied its waters, and at least thirteen sank in the river with remains visible at low-water events if you know where to look. At its mouth to the Gulf, the town of Velasco flourished as a trade center, one of the largest in the state, until it was wiped clean by a hurricane in 1875. It was not rebuilt on the shore. During and after the Civil War, railroads became more efficient methods of transportation and eventually replaced the riverboats. Lake Jackson Plantation, on an abandoned oxbow of the Brazos, was worked by slaves until the Civil War. After that time, Texas adopted a system of leasing state convicts to private companies to replace freed slaves. As many as thirty-six convicts worked this plantation between 1872 and 1884.

You can visit at least three Texas plantation homes from the times of the Austin Colony: the 1830s Henry Jones home at the George Ranch Historical Park; Varner Hogg Plantation Historical Park; and the plantation home of Anson Jones at Washington-on-the-Brazos State Historic Site. The Abner Jackson plantation is on Oyster Creek (plantation built in 1832; sugar mill in 1852). Texans declared their independence from Mexico on the banks of the Brazos at Washington-on-the-Brazos in 1836 after the Battle of the Alamo and before the Battle of San Jacinto.

The Brazos is the longest river in Texas between the Red River and the Rio Grande. John Graves's *Goodbye to a River* was written about its upper stretches (not covered in this guide). Both as literature and as the story of a river, this is a very good read. The TPWD's

Analysis of Texas Waterways dismisses the lower regions as "FM 979 to Gulf of Mexico. Not Mapped, 315 miles," "a very scenic coastal river. Here the stream slowly meanders to the Gulf between wide, steep banks. The banks are lined with hardwood trees and many scenic bluffs and sand bars exist. Water levels for recreational use are sufficient year round. Strong southerly winds can create problems for boaters at times." I take up where the *Analysis of Texas Waterways* leaves off, describing segments of those 315 miles. I have paddled several of these myself and concur with the "wide, steep banks . . . scenic bluffs and sand bars" and its susceptibility to wind effects. At least two rapids exist, and I will describe them in their respective sections. The descriptions start at the TX 21 crossing west of Bryan/College Station.

Brazos River

Access 1: TX 21 Crossing

This access point is about 10 miles west of Bryan/College Station. In December 2005 members of the Houston Canoe Club spent five days paddling the Brazos and camping out on sandbars, for a distance of about 53 miles. Typically for the Brazos, they had to scramble down unimproved steep banks to set off.

Even if you are not paddling, there are some other very interesting things to do at this crossing. A Houston Museum of Natural Science field trip guide describes it like this: "This locality is famous for being the 'most fossiliferous site in Texas.' It has been called 'Moseley Ferry' after the river crossing in the early days of Texas and more recently 'Whiskey Bridge' because this was the closest place to A&M where Aggies could go to get a drink. The fossils were first described in 1848 by Roemer, a German geologist sent by the Berlin Academy of Sciences to see if Texas was a fit place for a settlement." This field guide shows a variety of fossils from the ancient seas, including shark and gar teeth millions of years old.

Access 2: TX 60 Crossing

This is an unimproved access point about 15 miles downstream of the SH 21 crossing. TPWD does not list it, so it may be very rough indeed. People fish here, so there must be a route down to the bank where it may or may not be easy to take boats down to the water. Be sure to scout it before you attempt it. Even places that have relatively easy put-ins can be vastly altered by floods, which happen with some frequency on the Brazos. From the TX 60 crossing to the mouth of Yegua Creek is almost 32 miles; it is another 3.5 miles up Yegua Creek to where TX 50 crosses it. Yegua Creek is more usable as a put-in to paddle downstream.

Access 3: Yegua Creek

Yegua Creek is dammed to form Lake Somerville. The state park of the same name provides camping and boat access to this large lake. A new Texas State Paddling Trail is under development at Lake Somerville, so be sure to check the TPWD Web site (www.tpwd. state.tx.us/fishboat/boat/paddlingtrails/) for the latest information. From the Yegua's mouth on the Brazos to Hidalgo Falls is another 10 miles. About half of this distance the river will trend northeast along the face of the Hidalgo Bluffs to the south. You will then paddle almost due north for a mile and a half; as you follow a bend to the east, be on the lookout for the falls beyond the next bend. To get a bird's-eye view of this rapid, you can visit Steve Daniel's Web site (http:// philosophy.tamu.edu/~sdaniel/hidalgo.html) for photos and a thorough discussion of what to expect here at different water levels. The short story is to stay to the right on the right bend (west side of river) going into the rapid. Debris piles have formed at this rapid, which are potentially very dangerous—give them a wide berth.

If you have not joined the Texas River Protection Association (TRPA), you need to paddle another 5 miles downstream to the TX 105 crossing to take out. Only TRPA members can unlock the gates that give access to the river at Hidalgo Falls. About a mile downstream of the rapid you may see the concrete remains of a lock that was used to help steamboats get around the rapid by flooding to a depth where it no longer was an impediment.

Access 4: TX 105 Crossing

Access is from the highway right-of-way. The put-in is from an "unimproved," natural bank and can be very slippery and treacherous when it's been raining. About 3 miles past the bridge, and beyond where the Navasota River joins the Brazos, on the high bluff on your right is the Washington-on-the-Brazos State Historic Site. There is no access point from the park, and as you look up at it from the river, you probably don't even want to think about dragging a canoe, or yourself, up those tall, steep banks. Perhaps the nonpaddling members of your party will be enjoying a picnic under

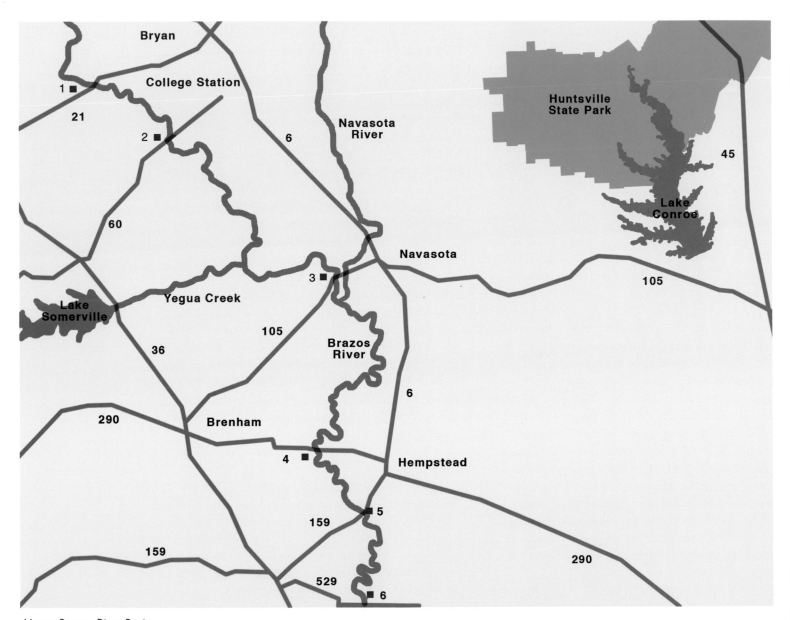

Upper Brazos River Basin

the pecan trees of the park and will give you a wave as you pass by. Be sure to bring plenty of food and water and good camping equipment for this stretch; it is at least 35 miles to the next access point. Have you wondered if there were any good overnight wilderness camping trips within easy driving distance of Houston? You will have plenty of nice white sandbars to choose from for campsites (unless, of course, the river is really up and roaring—in which case you probably don't want to be on it!). Islands are certainly in the public domain; if you wander far from the river, you are sure to be on private property. Take everything out that you packed in, and make sure your campfire is completely out. The next sign of "civilization" you will come to is US 290 near Hempstead.

Access 5: US 290 Crossing

Like the TX 159 crossing upstream, access here is from a paved turnaround under the bridge with a carry to the water. Heading downstream from 290 to the next crossing is about 18 miles.

Access Point 6: TX 159 Crossing

Both and north- and southbound approaches have paved access to under the bridge and unimproved access to the river. There are paths to the river and, for the Brazos, relatively easy access. The next crossing is 20 miles downstream.

Access 7: FM 529 Crossing

Just upstream of your destination at FM 1458 (15 miles) is the only other notable rapid on these stretches of the Brazos, known in the Houston Canoe Club as "Killer Fang." Occasionally the club runs trips (formal and informal) to put in at 1458 and paddle upstream to play in "Killer Fang" and practice moving-water maneuvers. The river makes a sharp left-hand turn over a rock ledge. You need to scout this before you plunge forward; there is good visibility from the right bank above the drop. A little farther upstream on the bluff above the river is Stephen F. Austin State Historic Park, which commemorates the area as the center of the "Old Three Hundred" Austin settlement

at San Felipe. This was an important fording place of the Atascocita Road before ferries and modern bridges.

Access 8: FM 1458 Crossing

The settlement of San Felipe, on the west bank of the Brazos River next to where present-day 1458 (formerly known as the Old San Antonio Road) crosses, was the unofficial capital of the Austin Colony at its founding in 1824. After the fall of the Alamo, Sam Houston's army retreated through San Felipe and burned the original town to the ground to prevent it from falling into the hands of the Mexican army. A reconstruction of part of that town and a museum are on-site today.

Both here and at the I-10 crossing you must negotiate a steep bank to put boats in or out of the water. At low-water levels, as in May 2011, the rocky bed of the Brazos is exposed and there are at least three whitewater rapids of Class I–II difficulty. There are also good fossil hunting and petrified wood on the large sandbars both upstream and downstream on this 6-mile stretch of the river, as well as an abandoned railroad bridge in the water.

Access 9: I-10 Crossing

This put-in is used by the Houston Geological Society and others for fossil-hunting trips. The trip description states: "This is the trip where you get to collect vertebrate fossils—bison, elephant, horse, camel, turtle, glyptodonts and others. There is also a whole lot of petrified wood. We may also see Indian arrow points, grinders, and anchors. . . . You will not need a hammer. You will get wet and muddy. This is the Brazos." The next crossing is 16.5 miles.

Access 10: FM 1093 Crossing

Access is from the marked "Canoe Launch Parking" area at the 1093 bridge. Members of Houston Canoe Club paddled the 51 miles from here to the US 90A bridge in Richmond, describing flocks of geese, ducks, cardinals, beavers, coyotes, and wild hogs on this stretch, as well as nice sandbar camping. The next crossing is 9 miles.

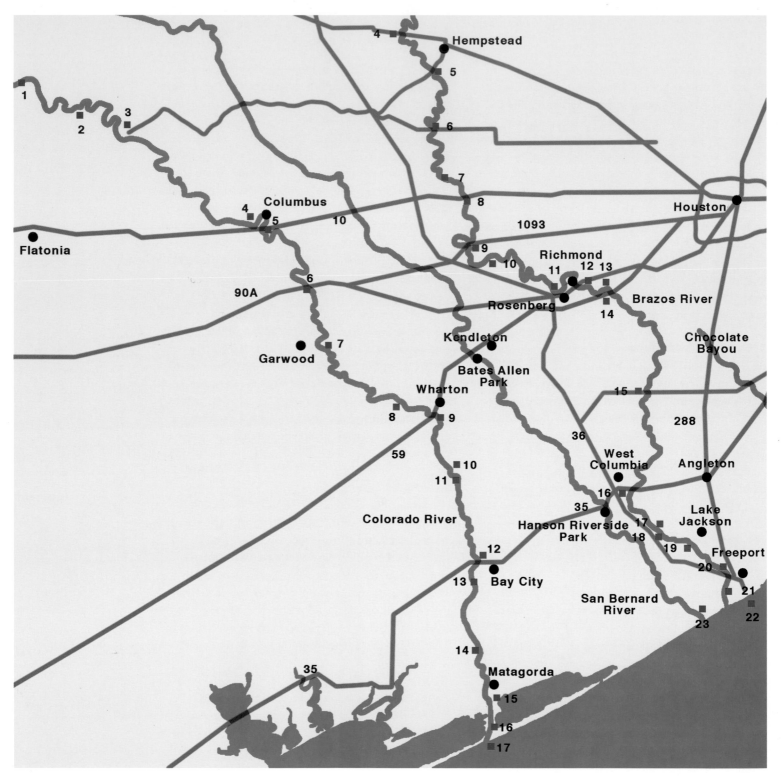

Brazos, Colorado, and San Bernard river basins

Access 11: FM 1489 Crossing

Access is from under the 1489 bridge, approaching from the north. The next crossing is 16.5 miles.

Access 12: FM 723 Crossing

About a third of the distance of the northern part of the loop is bounded to the south by George Park, but there does not appear to be any water access from this park. The distance and easy shuttle make this appear a good candidate for a day trip. However, experience with this stretch shows that both the Brazos Park (at the 723 crossing) and the US 90A accesses are very difficult, with steep banks and treacherous soft mud by the river. You will believe in the existence of quicksand if you spend much time along the banks of the Brazos. I certainly do.

At 723 there is a lot of concrete dumped over the riverbank that covers the soft mud, but the bank is too steep and uneven to make it easy to get a canoe and gear to the river. The river itself is quite nice between these two points, with sandbars and gravel bars after the first several miles and one riffle over a stone outcrop. The take-out was exhausting, with a struggle through soft mud before dragging all equipment up a long, steep bank. It is 9 miles to the next crossing, a horseshoe loop north of Richmond.

Access 13: US 90A Bridge

As described for access 12, this is a difficult put-in but only 6.5 river miles downstream to the newly built Grand Parkway, TX 99 bridge.

Access 14: Grand Parkway, TX 99 Crossing

The Brazos River flows through Sugar Land along a 9-mile corridor. The City has acquired approximately 1,200 acres of land along the banks of the river. Ultimately, the City hopes to own almost 3,600 acres for parks, open space, and conservation along the corridor.

The Brazos River Park will be developed over many years with multiple access points along the river, identified as subparks within the larger Brazos River Park. The park sites will provide access to trails, play areas, and the river as well as provide restrooms and picnic

facilities. Currently there is no access to the river at 99 or the proposed park site. It is 2.5 miles to the next access point, south at US 59.

Access 15: US 59 Bridge

You can park at the developing Sugar Land Memorial Park located at the intersection of University Boulevard and Commonwealth Boulevard—east bank of the Brazos south of the 59 crossing. Scout carefully before choosing your spot. The most gradual spot may be farther downstream but requires a long carry of your boat and equipment. Access to the river is from the northbound lanes of 59, with a parking area under the bridge. Although there is a paved turnaround under the bridge, access to the water is long and difficult. This long, unbroken stretch takes you 31 miles to the next crossing.

Access 16: FM 1462 Crossing

This leads to another uninterrupted, long stretch of 28 miles to the next crossing. If you decide you need another night of river camping before taking out at 1462, Brazos Bend State Park owns the property along the west bank, 2 to 3 miles upstream of 1462. Brazos Bend is known for its excellent birding, huge population of alligators, and the George Observatory, so it's well worth a visit if you have time. Unfortunately, canoes are not allowed on the water inside the park, and there does not appear to be any good access to Big Creek, which flows into the Brazos and might otherwise be a good access point from within the park.

Access 17: TX 35 Crossing

There is no apparent usable access to the river here. It is 10 miles to the next crossing.

Access 18: FM 521 Crossing

Scouting this on foot, I observed a lot of railroad traffic using the bridge just downstream of the highway bridge, with a historical marker on the importance of this bridge. There is probably a quarter mile of right-of-way frontage on the river, but a steep drop to the river, with trees or brambles to negotiate. At the water level that day, there was a 5-foot or more

Rocks and small rapids during low water on the Brazos

sheer drop from bank to river, a very treacherous, difficult way to get to the river. I suggest you paddle another 2.5 miles to the CR 849 boat ramp. For more history on the bridges on the Brazos, be sure to check out Jon McConal's book *Bridges over the Brazos*.

Access 19: CR 849 Public Boat Ramp

A few years ago I paddled this section to FM 2004 with my daughter and a friend. The Brazos had just come down from flood stage, so I experienced firsthand the silt load this river drops in as the water level decreases. The ramp was so full of knee-deep (and deeper as I got closer to the river) mud that I put my daughter in the bow of the boat and climbed in myself from 6 inches of mud; we slid down the muddy slope into the water, just as an otter would. There are many tales of quicksand and deep mud along the Brazos—believe it, and take this into

Steep Brazos River put-in at Richmond

An incredulous look from my daughter Ellen as we slide on a slurry of mud at CR 849 ramp

consideration if you are paddling after a flooding event.

This is a one-lane boat ramp. Be sure to park out of the way and well up the hill so that fishers can get their boats in and out of the water without having to weave around your vehicle. The 8.5 miles from here to the Buffalo Camp Bayou go by very quickly—be sure to look along the left bank of the river for the bayou's entrance; the boat ramp is out of sight and upstream in the bayou.

Access 20: Buffalo Camp Bayou Boat Ramp

This access is near the FM 2004 crossing. If you arrive at the 2004 bridge from upstream, you have gone too far; turn around, paddle back upstream, and look for the bayou's entrance on the right (east) side of the river about a quarter mile upstream. There are multiple ramps for motorboats to get in or out of the water on their trailers, and a very large paved parking area—I wish all access points were this convenient! The ramp is on the east side of the Brazos and north of 2004—look for the brown sign off the side road that will take you to it. There is a restroom building here, but I am not sure it is functional.

When I paddled the segment above here, the boat ramp had not been built and the takeout was very difficult, requiring a scramble up and over the steep riverbank and concrete embankment. As you head back to Houston on 2004, shortly after the intersection with TX 332 to the north side of the road, you will see signs for Abner Jackson's plantation on the oxbow lake to the north, which gave the town of Lake Jackson its name. It is open only the first Saturday of the month at this time but is obviously being reconstructed, and you might expect more visiting times in the future.

Access 21: TX 36 Crossing

From southbound TX 36, exit right before crossing the Brazos River. The concrete ramp is under the bridge on the east side of the river and has lots of parking available. This and the two access points north are used by trailered boats, so expect increasing numbers of motorboats as you head farther south on the Brazos. If you want to paddle from here to the last ramp along the Brazos, it is about another 4 miles.

Access 22: CR 242A (Levee Road) Public Boat Ramp

Although you are still a mile from the Gulf, you have driven as far as you can, with the ICW between you and the farthest tip of land on the Gulf. To get to this point from TX 36, on the east side of its crossing the Brazos, go south on CR 242A (Levee Road). The road will end at the public boat ramp.

Access 23: Quintana Beach

If you are insistent on paddling into the Gulf, you can paddle past the boat ramp at access 22, turn east when you come to the Gulf, and in about 6 miles you will reach the public beach at Quintana Beach Park and Pier.

▲◄ Collapsed banks of the Brazos River

▲ Stepped banks of the Brazos River

◄ Mark Andrus floating down the muddy Brazos River

Sand mining along the Brazos River

Access 24: San Bernard River Boat Ramp

Another alternative to a beach or ICW paddle to the east from access 22 is to head west to the mouth of the San Bernard River at the southern terminus of CR 2918. This is about 6 miles beyond access 22.

Navasota River

The Navasota River flows for 125 miles to meet the Brazos River near Washington-on-the-Brazos State Historic Site, on the west bank of the Brazos at the confluence.

There is a relatively easy access to the river from the TX 30 crossing east of Bryan/College Station. USGS gage 08110800 gives good indication of whether or not you can paddle very far without dragging your canoe or kayak over sandbars: at a reading of 100 cfs and above, this is a pleasant paddle; if the reading is above 1,000 cfs, consider the river in flood. At flows significantly less than 100 cfs, the river will shallow out and not have enough water to float your canoe for a long distance. The river is relatively narrow and heavily wooded, so trees in the water can block your travel up- or downstream. Heading downstream is about 20 miles to the next take-out spot, so this is not a recommended stretch for an easy day paddle but has potential for an overnight trip.

TX 6 is the next river crossing. From the southbound lanes there is dirt-road, unimproved access to the river. The road can be deeply rutted so is not recommended in wet weather and should be scouted before attempting to drive. In another 8 miles TX 105 crosses, and 5 miles downstream the Navasota River flows into the Brazos River. There is no river access at that location; you would have to paddle several miles upstream on the Brazos to its 105 crossing; it is better to take out from the Navasota River at its 105 crossing. The Navasota is accessed from TX 105 from the eastbound lanes, west bank of the river. None of these access points have amenities.

Facilities

Brazos River Basin

Paddling area	Access point	Toilet	Picnic	Camping	Water	Ramp	Parking	Gage	Mileage	Comments
Brazos River										
	Access 1: TX 21 crossing					●	●	08108700	15	
	Access 2: TX 60 crossing					●			20	
	Access 3: Yegua Creek	●	●	●	●	●	●	08109700	35	Lake Somerville State Park
	Access 4: TX 105 crossing								35	
	Access 5: US 290 crossing							08111500	18	
	Access 6: TX 159 crossing								20	
	Access 7: FM 529 crossing								15	
	Access 8: FM 1458 crossing								6	
	Access 9: I-10 crossing								16.5	
	Access 10: FM 1093 crossing								9	
	Access 11: FM 1489 crossing								16.5	
	Access 12: FM 723 crossing		●				●		9	Brazos Park; very difficult river access
	Access 13: US 90A bridge							08114000	6.5	Difficult access
	Access 14: Grand Parkway, TX 99 crossing								2.5	
	Access 15: US 59 bridge								31	
	Access 16: FM 1462 crossing							08116650	28	
	Access 17: TX 35 crossing								10	Extreme difficulty; not recommended
	Access 18: FM 521 crossing								2.5	
	Access 19: CR 849 public boat ramp					●			8.5	
	Access 20: Buffalo Camp Bayou boat ramp					●	●		9.5	
	Access 21: TX 36 crossing					●	●		4	
	Access 22: CR 242A (Levee Road) public boat ramp					●	●		6	
	Access 23: Quintana Beach								6	
	Access 24: San Bernard River boat ramp					●	●			
Navasota River								08110800	13	
	TX 30 crossing								20	
	TX 6 crossing								8	
	TX 105 crossing								5	

8 San Bernard River Basin

AT THEIR LOWER PASSAGES, the Brazos, San Bernard, and Colorado rivers flow in parallel to the Gulf of Mexico, hardly 50 miles apart. The San Bernard is the shortest of the three rivers, about 120 miles in total length. Its smaller drainage area means that upper reaches are sometimes dry and not paddleable. The portion that has water most of the year begins around the US 59 crossing near Kendleton in Fort Bend County. The Advanced Hydrologic Prediction Service on the Web has a gage located near Sweeney that works when the river is above minimal levels. At the lower end of the river is the more than 20,000-acre San Bernard National Wildlife Refuge.

San Bernard River

The San Bernard more closely resembles a lake than a river at this location but has a nice access point.

Access 1: Bates Allen County Park

This is just east of where US 59 crosses the river, at 630 Charlie Roberts Lane. There are walking trails, a play area, a fishing pier, restrooms, and a canoe ramp. The direct access to the San Bernard River is on a stretch known as the "Blue Hole" where the river is backed up from a dam of downed trees downstream. The Blue Hole is actually a spring that feeds the river. There are several miles of lake to paddle here—where the river narrows and passes into the trees, I suggest you turn around and head back upstream. Reports that I have seen, and my personal experience from putting in some miles downstream of here, confirm the periodic disappearance and reappearance of the river in mega logjams. Don't plan on running south from this point unless you really like bushwhacking, log jumping, and carrying your boat through thick underbrush.

Access 2: Hanson Riverside Park

This is very close to the TX 35 crossing. Brown park signs mark the turn to Hanson Riverside County Park from TX 35. You will find plenty of parking here, picnic and restroom facilities, and a pleasant walking trail down an oak allée at the far end of the park. That trail is gated, so you cannot drive the 200 yards to a gradual ramp to the water. For information, call the Brazoria County Parks Department (979-864-1541). You can paddle upstream for several miles to a saltwater barrier; the freshwater backed up to the upstream side is for use of the Conoco Phillips refinery. If you are so inclined (and I don't recommend it), you can paddle the approximately 50 miles from here to the Gulf of Mexico. FM 522 crosses about 5 miles downstream, but since its sign states "authorized boats only," boat launching is discouraged. The public boat ramp at FM 521 is about 18 miles downstream from Hanson Riverside Park.

Access 3: FM 521 Public Boat Ramp

From here it is about 8 miles downstream to the public boat ramp at FM 2004 (or 2611), with a crossing by CR 310 a mile or so upstream of 2004. You will see a lot of fish camps and homes along the river as it passes through the coastal prairies.

Access 4: FM 2004 (or 2611) Boat Ramp

You have another 15 miles to go to the "end of the line" on the river, where it makes a T-intersection into the ICW. You are truly into the coastal marshes here, with a strip of private land and CR 2918 between you and the San Bernard National Wildlife Refuge to your west. Most boaters in this area are running with a motor because there are some commercial access points along here and more places to put a motorboat in the water or take it out.

Access 5: CR 2918 Public Boat Ramp

This ramp has historically been a launching place for the sea-kayaking crowd to paddle into the Gulf and then to find a private sandy beach for overnight camping. The ramp itself is on the ICW, so if you are paddling downstream on the San Bernard, make sure you make that right-hand turn (westward) onto the ICW to find the ramp.

Thanks to tropical storms and other weather events, the mouth of the San Bernard to the Gulf was filled in by sand deposits. Its waters spilled into the ICW and made treacherous navigation problems for commercial barge traffic and blocked access to the Gulf for folks in smaller boats. The Gulf entrance was dredged in 2009, once again allowing access. The photo shows the sandbar before dredging operations.

Cedar Lakes

Exploration of the Cedar Lakes area is a nice side trip. During a paddle on a cool winter day the water was low enough to expose hundreds of oysters, some spitting and opening and closing their shells. Apparently roseate spoonbills find this to their liking, too, as they have a fairly permanent rookery in the area.

Lower San Bernard River

Where the San Bernard meets the Gulf of Mexico before the cut was reopened

Caney Creek

Caney Creek empties into the Gulf between the San Bernard and Colorado rivers. Like the other streams in the region, it was used in the past to transport cotton and agricultural goods between the plantations and markets. The part described begins with a fringe of woodland and ends in the coastal marshes. My familiarity with it is as a fund-raiser kayak run for the Sargent Public Library. Although it is called a "kayak fest," I have run it each year in a canoe and you can, too.

Both put-in and take-out points are commercial ventures: Caney Creek RV Park and take-out at Caney Creek Marina. The run between these two points is listed as 9 miles; it seemed longer than that to me because I encountered really strong headwinds the second half of the run both times I paddled it.

Access 1: Caney Creek RV Park
■ *Paddling Note.* To get to Caney Creek RV Park, take FM 457 south from Sargent. As the road bends to the right (east), make the first right turn (just past the

Roseate spoonbill rookery at Cedar Lakes. Photo by Bruce Bodson

bend) on Lillian Lane. Not far down that road you will see the Caney Creek RV Park sign; turn right and go down to the ramp. There is a fee to use the ramp; call 979-245-4735 for more information.

Access 2: Caney Creek Marina

■ *Paddling Note.* Take FM 457 south from Sargent, and follow it toward Sargent Beach (if you miss all the next turns, you dead-end right on the beach); go right again in about 5 miles on Carancahua Street, and look for the Caney Creek Marina on your right.

This is also a commercial boat ramp, and you will see lots of motorized craft putting in or taking out there. There is a fee here, too, and pretty good seafood available right next to the ramp. If you decide you would really like to spend some time on the beach, follow 457 to its end. The beach is complete with paved parking and a picnic area to the west along the beach road.

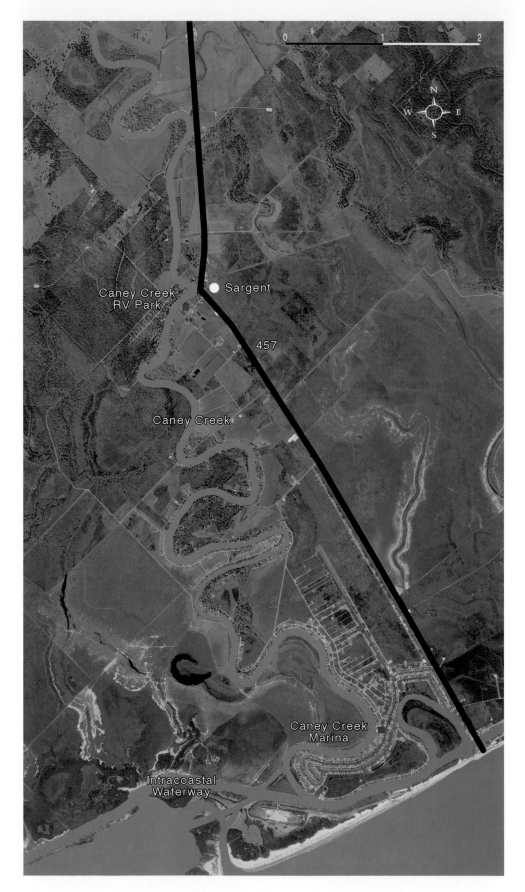

Caney Creek

Facilities

San Bernard River Basin

Paddling area	Access point	Toilet	Picnic	Camping	Water	Ramp	Parking	Gage	Mileage	Comments
San Bernard River								08117500		Gage at Boling (20 miles upriver)
	Access 1: Bates Allen County Park	●	●			●	●		2	
	Access 2: Hanson Riverside Park	●	●		●		●			
	Access 3: FM 521 public boat ramp					●	●		8	
	Access 4: FM 2004 (o 2611) public boat ramp r					●	●		15	
	Access 5: CR 2918 public boat ramp					●	●		5	
Cedar Lakes										
Caney Creek										
	Access 1: Caney Creek RV Park	●	●	●	●	●	●		10	Fee
	Access 2: Caney Creek Marine	●		●	●	●	●			Fee

9   Colorado River Basin

THE FIRST EUROPEAN to visit the Colorado River was Alonso Álvarez de Pineda, who mapped the Texas coastline in 1519. Álvar Núñez Cabeza de Vaca crossed the Matagorda Peninsula to explore the inland area after 1528. The French explorer René-Robert Cavelier, Sieur de La Salle lost his ship *La Belle* in the bay in1686. The *La Belle* was rediscovered and excavated in 1996.

The first Anglo settlers arrived after 1820 as a part of Stephen F. Austin's colony at the mouth of the Colorado. Austin gave grants in the area to fifty-two families and in 1827 received permission to settle three hundred more within 30 leagues of the coast. The town of Matagorda, at the mouth of the Colorado, was founded in 1829 when Austin convinced the Mexican government that a military post was needed to protect incoming settlers. Rice, cotton, and sugarcane were important to early settlers and are grown today along the lower reaches of the Colorado.

The town of Columbus, first known as Beeson's Ford, was started by the Austin colonists. Austin had intended to locate his headquarters here and laid out a town in 1823 but changed the headquarters to a more promising location on the Brazos, probably as a result of frequent Indian attacks and poor drainage.

In 1934 the Colorado River Authority was formed as a conservation and reclamation district and is split into three divisions: upper, middle, and lower. It is the jurisdiction of the Lower Colorado River Authority (LCRA) that is covered in this guide. The LCRA supplies low-cost electricity for Central Texas, manages water supplies and controls floods in the lower Colorado River basin, develops water and wastewater utilities, provides public parks, and supports community and economic development in fifty-eight Texas counties. The LCRA owns about 16,000 acres of recreational lands along the Highland Lakes and Colorado River. The coverage of the Colorado River for purposes of this guide begins at Smithville and continues downstream. The LCRA launched the Colorado River Trail program in 1992 and has developed very good guides to the river and quite a few access points and trails.

Colorado River

Access 1: Vernon L. Richards Riverbend Park

Vernon L. Richards Riverbend Park is operated by the City of Smithville. In addition to river access, the park offers overnight camping, picnic tables, potable water, and restrooms. It is 17 miles from here to the next access point at Plum Park, operated by the LCRA. The LCRA includes a map of this stretch of the river and describes the first leg of this two-day trip on its Web site (www.lcra.org/community/ecodev/crt/crt_river3.html for map; www.lcra.org/community/ecodev/crt/two_day_float.html for trip):

For the experienced canoeist, this trip demands advanced planning, fitness and endurance. The challenging trip covers 35 miles of river between Smithville and LaGrange. Be prepared for two full days of physical recreation, with everything from deep, quiet pools to frothy white riffles.

Archaeologists have found evidence that this stretch of the Colorado was used by bison and elephant-like mastodons, now extinct. Diaries from early French explorers chronicle losing one of their colleagues to a hungry alligator. River regulars catch channel catfish and freshwater drum on earthworms, or bass and bluegill on small in-line spinners.

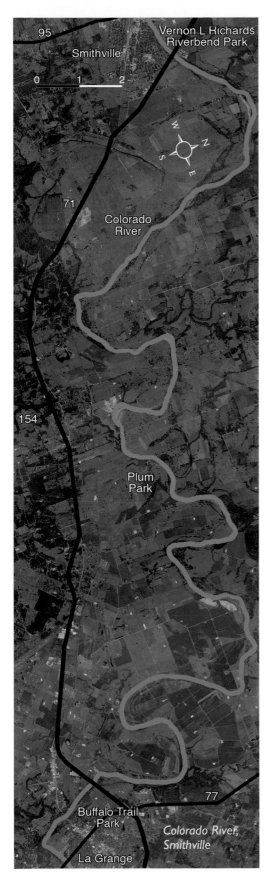

Colorado River, Smithville

Access 2: Plum Park

➡ *Directions.* Plum Park is accessed from Prairie Valley Road, heading east from TX 71 about 10 miles north of La Grange, or 3 miles south of the intersection of 71 and TX 154. It is a day-use park with waterless toilets and picnic tables, but no potable water. Overnight camping is allowed without a permit for people arriving by river. For those arriving by car or groups of more than twenty people, an overnight camping permit may be arranged by calling 800-776-5272 or e-mailing parkinfo@lcra.org.

For many years the Alamo City Rivermen have put on a "Freeze Trip" that attracts a very large number of participants from across the state, including many from the Houston area. It is typically run in late January, and the "freeze" part of the trip has certainly been known to occur. Participants put in at Plum Park and use this stretch for a relatively easy two-day trip. Some miles into the trip is a large island with a rocky beach and space for the twenty to fifty or more participants to pitch tents and set up a huge Dutch oven cook-off

Mary Zaborowski on a Freeze Trip, with the ultimate canoe-campers' cooking setup. Photo by Sharon Anderson

THE HOUSTON CANOE CLUB TRIP of May 30, 2005, had more than fifty paddlers on the river in all kinds of craft: canoes were predominant, but there were whitewater kayaks, sit-on-top kayaks, sea kayaks, and inflatable kayaks with one, two, or three people in each craft. The heavy downpour that I encountered south of Houston on my way to the river thankfully stayed to the south and east; the light overcast kept the temperatures down to a comfortable high of 82. The winds died down. They can be a real hazard on a river this wide and open, so conditions were nearly ideal for paddling. The water temperature was very pleasant, probably in the mid- or upper 70s.

At least three places gave novice paddlers trouble. As I approached the first spot just behind the trip leaders, I eddied out and walked back upstream a short distance on a rock to keep the group on my side of the river—undercut trees on the far bank were a definite hazard. As we came to an island, most of the group went left where we could see the route was unobstructed; I went for the right channel around the island and found impressive whirlpools at the bottom of the riffle. The next challenging spot had a right turn at the bottom of a chute—and again, trees overhanging the water. This time my daughter and her friends were ahead of me and beyond reach of my motherly advice. Next thing I knew, I saw the canoe roll over against the branches, and all three girls swimming beside it. Thankfully, they did a mostly self-rescue with a chase of free-floating belongings and a good laugh for the adventure. Several others of the group bounced off the trees, but no more rolled over.

While the girls got their possessions and boat back together, the group took a break, including a swim, at the gravel- and sandbar just downstream. Paddling onward, we took a short side trip up Cummins Creek where it comes in from river left (east bank). Big trees practically touch overhead; it's a much more sheltered area than the open river. Not far below that is another constricted area in the river. By this time the sweep boat had caught all of us and was sitting in the eddy just below the drop. The rest of us proceeded on downstream another mile or two. The chosen lunch spot was about another mile along, perhaps mile 5 of the 6-mile trip. We set up on another very large gravel bar, with the shade of trees, for our repast. As we were packing to leave, finally the sweep boat pulled into view again, with several other canoes. Their late arrival unfortunately resulted because another boat had had a major mishap upstream and was pinned against a tree in a very bad spot—its two occupants had to ride with other paddlers to this point and lost their lunches and everything else in the boat.

In a mile the take-out is unmistakably marked by two bridges crossing the river. First there is a railroad bridge with a lot of detritus in the water beneath it. Below that is the green highway bridge crossing to Beason Park, on the left bank of the river. Take out just beyond the second bridge. Of my group, all three girls and a young man chose to swim from the lunch spot to the take-out. At only a few spots could they touch the bottom, but it was a nice easy ride in a PFD.

Houston Canoe Club on the Columbus Loop. Photo by John Bartos

led by Mary Zaborowski, Houston Canoe Club camp cook extraordinaire.

Although the LCRA describes this stretch of the river as relatively obstruction-free, when I have paddled it, in this stretch and the one at Columbus, the river flows over a rocky bed and there are riffles and Class I "rapids" that will make a believer of the unwary with little control of their boats or inability to read moving water. The next access is 18 miles.

Access 3: Buffalo Trail Park, La Grange

The park is located directly under the Business 71 bridge at the spot where an old buffalo trail, which became part of the La Bahia road, crossed the Colorado River. The park has a paved boat ramp and parking area and picnic tables. If you are putting in here, it is a very long stretch to the next access point near Columbus—at least 30 miles long with no public access points. Presumably there will be island and sandbar camping sites available for a multiday trip, but I don't know that with certainty.

Access 4: Highway 71 Crossing, the "Columbus Loop"

➡ *Directions.* From I-10 west of Houston, exit at Business 71. Head north through the town of Columbus. You will shortly cross the river; slow down to turn right from the highway and make a U-turn to go down to the put-in, which is practically under the bridge you just crossed. The shuttle to your take-out is only 1.5 miles, and for that short shuttle, you will have 6 miles of paddling on an enormous bend as the river heads first north, then east, south, west, and south again. For the shuttle, follow Business 71 back through town, by the courthouse, and make a left turn (east) on US 90. Once again you will cross the river; make a right turn, this time into Beason Park. There is plenty of parking space here and a gradual slope down to the river from which you will be carrying boats back up to your vehicles for the trip home.

This 6-mile stretch of river is easy to access and a very pleasant float with an easy shuttle. It is a favorite of the Houston Canoe Club and the location of several "buddy paddles" where members invite friends

Island camping on the Colorado River. Photo by Marilyn Kircus

and family for an introduction to canoeing. It is about 70 miles from Houston so a little farther than several other trips described here, but it is easy to get there and worth the extra drive.

■ *Paddling Note.* The banks of the river are quite steep in some places, and in others there are sandy and sometime pebbly beaches. Water flows may average about 1,200 cfs. For gaging information, go to the USGS Web site (waterdata.usgs.gov/tx/nwis/current/?type=flow; enter gage site number, 08161000) and check for "Colorado River at Columbus." The gage is directly opposite the take-out at Beason Park. This is a broad river with a few places where the current rushes over sandbars or pebbles; trees are not uncommon hazards in the water, and when you get close to the end, beware of construction rubble in the water. At lower levels, large sandbars are exposed and make nice stopping places.

Access 5: Beason Park

➡ *Directions.* To get to this park from I-10, take Exit 698 and follow US 90 to Columbus. The park will be on your left before you cross the river; turn in and

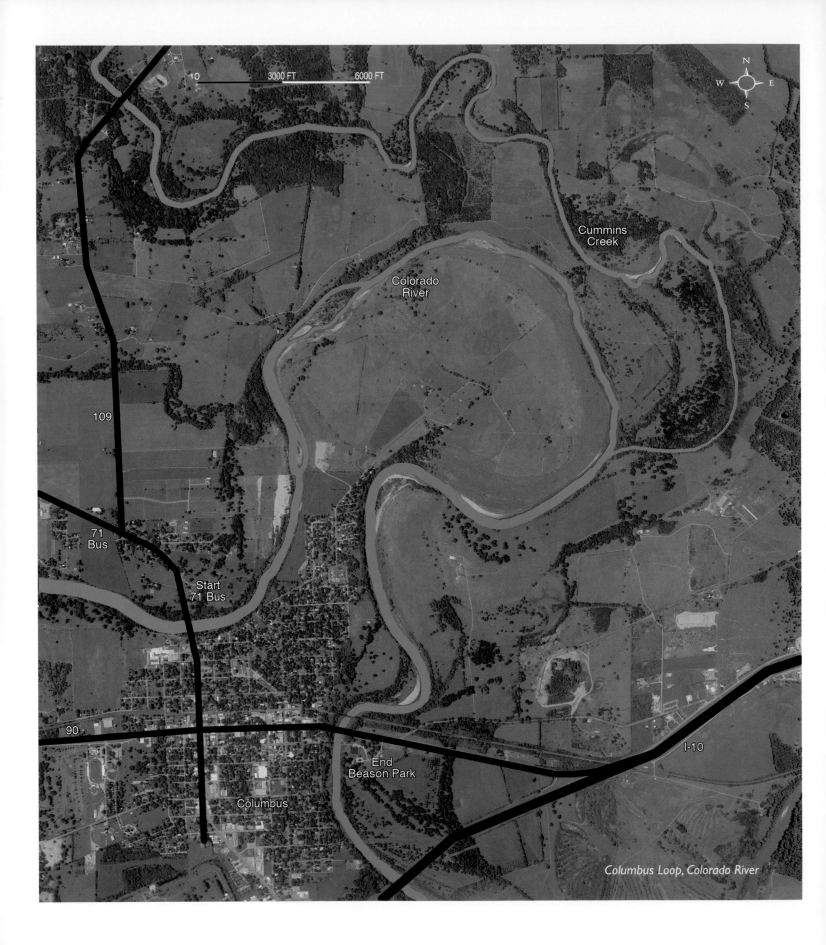

0   3000 FT   6000 FT

N
W · E
S

Cummins
Creek

Colorado
River

109

71
Bus

Start
71 Bus

90

End
Beason Park

I-10

Columbus

Columbus Loop, Colorado River

follow the road to its closest approach to the water near the bridge. You will need to carry your boat and gear about 100 yards to the water. The next access point is 12 miles from here.

Access 6: Altair Boat Ramp

Altair boat ramp and picnic facilities are located on the north side of US 90A 3 miles east of Altair. It is about 20 miles to the next access point. Beware the Garwood dam; portage it on river left.

Access 7: FM 950 Crossing at Garwood

There is a nice place to park your car, but a slide of about 20 feet to the point where you can access the river.

■ *Paddling Note.* Several years ago, Marilyn Kircus and I decided to explore this stretch of the river using her 18-foot-long ultralightweight tandem canoe. Her car was left at this location; mine was left as a shuttle car at the next crossing 22 miles downstream. Some kids entertained themselves by scratching marks all over Marilyn's car while their father fished and paid no attention to them. We did this stretch in one day— not what I would recommend for the fainthearted or someone who doesn't want to paddle hard for hours. We enjoyed beautiful big sandbars and observed the erosion power of the river that had left fence lines dangling in the air where once there had been high riverbanks. Our best finds were traces of critters walking across the sandbars, big beautiful freshwater shells, and what appeared to be vertebrae of long-gone dinosaurs now poking through the sand. The sand beaches were ours alone for lunch and paddle breaks, and the light north wind of the day pushed us along as supplement to our tandem double-bladed paddle power. It was an absolutely beautiful day on the river.

Access 8: FM 960 Crossing at Glen Flora

This access has a steep put-in or take-out but otherwise is a wide, grassy parking area for accessing the river. From here it is a relatively short 7.5 miles to the next access point.

Fence dangling in midair where the bank used to be along the Colorado River. Photo by Marilyn Kircus

Access 9: US 90A Crossing West of Wharton

Beware the Lane City dam—portage on river right. It is about 8 miles into this 10-mile stretch of water.

Access 10: Lane City Dam

Access is via CR 120, heading west from TX 60 at Lane City. From here it is a short hop to Hollywood Bottom Park, about 3 miles downstream.

Access 11: Hollywood Bottom Park

This park offers picnic sites, a sandy beach, toilets, and a canoe launch site. It is open for camping, but groups numbering more than twenty must have a permit. Call 800-776-5272 for permits. It is about 18 miles from here to the next crossing (west of Bay City).

You will notice large caution/warning signs just below the TX 35 bridge concerning the dam 1 mile downstream. Although you can portage at the dam, it is a long way around the dam, so you are better off taking out at the 35 bridge.

Access 12: TX 35 Crossing

This is a take-out spot for the upper stretch of river, not recommended as a put-in because of the large dam 1 mile downstream. However, if you would like to paddle on the lake created by the dam, you can put in and take out from this same spot. Be very cautious about getting close to the dam, and do use the recommended portage route. Look for signs.

Access 13: Riverside Park

Riverside Park is located at 7330 FM 2668 about 3 miles south of Bay City. The access road to the park is 2 miles long, and the entrance is well marked with a "Rio Colorado Golf Course and Riverside Park" sign on 2668. This park was opened in 1993 and has full-hookup campsites, a paved boat ramp, a picnic pavilion for groups, and other amenities. It is operated by the City of Bay City. A day-use fee is required; call the park at 979-245-0340 for reservations and information. There is a nice boat ramp in the park on a large

sandbar. No lifeguard is posted on this sandbar/beach, which would certainly be tempting as a swimming spot. In addition to the full-hookup campsites, there are some with water and electricity only, and a large group site. The camping area is well shaded with large oak trees. This is a good launching spot to run 12 miles of river to the next access point.

Access 14: FM 521 Crossing

River Park is located where FM 521 crosses near the town of Wadsworth and is maintained by Matagorda County. It has picnic sites, a group pavilion, a fishing pier, and a boat ramp. For more information, call the County at 361-972-2719. The next access point is 8 miles downriver.

Access 15: River Bend Boat Ramp

There are at least three commercial (for fee) boat ramps close to the crossing of the Colorado River and the ICW. The ramps farthest north require you to head east up the ICW; C and R Marina is the first you will come to (check TGLO's *Texas Beach and Bay Access Guide*); Matagorda Harbor is farther east along the ICW; and to get to the River Bend Tavern and Marina, you will have to head south again on what may be an old channel of the Colorado. If you stay on the main channel of the Colorado without making the ICW turn, there are several marinas/boat slips along FM 2031. From the ICW it is about 7 miles to the Gulf of Mexico.

Access 16: Matagorda Bay Nature Park

There is a brand-new Nature Center at Matagorda Bay Nature Park with classrooms, nature and science exhibits, and a for-fee RV park with seventy sites. Kayak rentals are available at the RV Park. Access is from FM 2031 on the east side of the river. A 2.5-mile kayak trail is open to guided kayaking trips, which can be arranged by calling the LCRA at McKinney Roughs (800-776-5272, ext. 8021). Camping is also allowed on the beach for a fee.

Matagorda Bay Nature Park

Facilities

Colorado River Basin

Paddling area	Access point	Toilet	Picnic	Camping	Water	Ramp	Parking	Gage	Mileage	Commentse
Colorado River										
	Access 1: Vernon L. Richards Riverbend Park	●	●	●	●	●	●	08159500	17	
	Access 2: Plum Park	●	●	●			●	08160400	18	
	Access 3: Buffalo Trail Park, La Grange		●			●	●		30	
	Access 4: TX 71 crossing, the "Columbus Loop"								6	
	Access 5: Beason Park	●	●	●	●		●	08161000	12	
	Access 6: Altair boat ramp		●			●	●		20	
	Access 7: FM 950 crossing at Garwood								22	
	Access 8: FM 960 crossing at Glen Flora								7.5	
	Access 9: US 90A crossing west of Wharton							08162000	10	Dam must be portaged
	Access 10: Lane City dam								3	Long, steep bank to river
	Access 11: Hollywood Bottom Park		●	●	●				18	Steep banks
	Access 12: TX 35 crossing							08162500		Not recommended
	Access 13: Riverside Park	●	●	●	●		●		12	
	Access 14: FM 521 crossing		●			●	●		8	River Park
	Access 15: River Bend boat ramp					●	●		7	Fee
	Access 16: Matagorda Bay Nature Park	●		●	●				2.5	

Appendix

Organizations That May Put You on the Water

This list of profit and not-for-profit organizations offers a variety of services that will help you get started in paddling or broaden your horizons. This is not a strict endorsement; these are groups that I know about and that have been known to put boats and people on the water. There are sure to be others, but these can help you get started.

Armand Bayou Nature Center: 8500 Bay Area Boulevard, Pasadena. For a fee, the Nature Center sponsors canoe trips and pontoon boat tours on Armand Bayou. Web site: www.abnc.org. Phone: 281-474-2551.

Artist Boat: 2415 Avenue K, Galveston. Education-based awareness and recreation of the coastal margins and marine environment. Web site: www.artistboat.org. Phone: 409-770-0722.

Austin Canoe and Kayak: 5822 Bissonnet, Houston. A specialty retailer that sells canoes and kayaks and has an active interest in kayak fishing. Web site: www.austinkayak.com. Phone: 713-660-7000 or toll free, 888-828-3826.

Bayou Preservation Association: 3201 Allen Parkway, Suite 200, near Buffalo Bayou in downtown Houston. Offers pontoon boat and canoe and kayak tours of area bayous, Buffalo Bayou in particular. Web site: www.bayoupreservation.org. Phone: 713-752-0314.

Buffalo Bayou Shuttle Service: Offers tours, rentals, and, as the name implies, shuttle services for Buffalo Bayou. Web site: www.bayoushuttle.com. Phone: 713-538-7433.

Camp Mohawk County Park: Alvin, Brazoria County. Has a canoe and kayak program starting up. Web site: www.brazoria-county.com/parks/Mohawk/index.html. Phone: 281-581-2319.

Jesse H. Jones Park and Nature Center: Harris Country Precinct 4 park in Humble. Offers guided canoe trips on Spring Creek. Web site: www.hcp4.net/jones/index.htm. Phone: 281-446-8588.

Lower Colorado River Authority: Headquarters at 3700 Lake Austin Boulevard, Austin. Offers river trips on upper stretches (north of the area covered by this guide) and kayak tours of Matagorda Bay Nature Park. Web site: www.lcra.org. Phone: toll free, 800-776-5272 ext. 4740.

North Lake Conroe Paddling Company: 13988 Calvary Road, Willis, north of Houston. Has boats for rent as well as instruction and tours. Web site: www.northlakeconroepaddlingco.com. Phone: 936-203-2697.

REI (Recreation Equipment Incorporated): Two locations in Houston, one at the Willowbrook Mall (832-237-8833) and one at 7538 Westheimer (713-353-2582). Outdoor supply company that sells and rents canoes and kayaks and sponsors programs about paddling, paddle places, and "try out" days when you can actually paddle REI's line of boats on the water. Web site: www.rei.com.

Southwest Paddlesports: 26322 I-45 North, Spring (in The Woodlands). Sells boats and equipment, teaches lessons, leads tours, and rents kayaks and canoes. Web site: www.paddlesports.com. Phone: 281-292-5600 or toll free, 800-937-2335.

Whitewater Experience: 6005 Cypress Street, Houston. Despite the name, the company does plenty of training and trips on flatwater in the Houston area and offers classes, rentals, and trips both near and far. Web site: www.whitewaterexperience.com. Phone: 713-774-1028.

References

Antrobus, Sally E. 2005. *Galveston Bay*. College Station: Texas A&M University Press.

Arthur, Bob. 2003. "Burnam's Ferry Exploration Trip." *WaterLine* [newsletter of Houston Canoe Club] 25 (March). [Many issues of *WaterLine* were consulted. For a complete run, go to the Houston Canoe Club Web site, www.houstoncanoeclub.org and click on "newsletter."]

Aulbach, Louis. 2012. *Buffalo Bayou, an Echo of Houston's Wilderness Beginnings*. Houston: Louis F. Aulbach.

Bartos, John R. 2001. "Colorado River at Pierce Ranch." *WaterLine* [newsletter of Houston Canoe Club] 11 (December): 1–2.

Blackburn, Jim. 2004. *The Book of Texas Bays*. College Station: Texas A&M University Press.

Clay, John V. 1987. *Spain, Mexico, and the Lower Trinity: An Early History of the Texas Gulf Coast*. Baltimore: Gateway Press.

Crawford, Ray. 2003. *Wade and Kayak Fishing on Galveston Bay and Surrounding Areas*. 3rd ed. Friendswood: Texas Coastal Fishing Books.

Explorer's Guide: Colorado River Trail. 2003. Austin: Lower Colorado River Authority.

Fehrenbach, T. R. 1968. *Lone Star: A History of Texas and the Texans*. New York: Macmillan.

Fleischman, Flavia Stuffs. [1976] 1999. *Old River Country: A History of West Chambers County*. Reprint, Baltimore: Gateway Press.

Galveston Bay Foundation. 1998. *Galveston Bay Habitat Conservation Blueprint: A Plan to Restore the Habitats and Heritage of Galveston Bay: Sites, Strategies, and Resources*. Webster, TX: Galveston Bay Foundation.

Garg, Gaurav. 2004. "Quantifying Long Term Changes in the Streamflow Characteristics in Texas." Master's thesis, Texas A&M University.

Gonzalez, Lisa, and Bradley Christoffersen, eds. 2006. *The Quiet Invasion: A Guide to Invasive Species of the Galveston Bay Area*. www.galvbayinvasives.org.

Google Earth. http://earth.google.com. [Aerial photography facilitates "scouting" from the desktop.]

Great Texas Coastal Birding Trail: Upper Texas Coast. 2002. 2nd ed. Austin: Texas Parks and Wildlife, Texas Department of Transportation.

Guthrie, Keith. 1988–95. *Texas Forgotten Ports*. 4 vols. Austin: Eakin Press.

Handbook of Texas Online. www.tsha.utexas.edu/handbook/online/.

Henson, Margaret Swetts. 1988. *Chambers County: A Pictorial History*. Norfolk, VA: Donning.

Holtkamp, Wendee. 2006. "Delta Dawn: The Young Colorado River Delta Is a Lush Breeding Ground for Finfish, Shrimp, Crab, and Controversy." *Texas Parks and Wildlife Magazine* 64 (7): 50–55.

Houston Atlas of Biodiversity: Houston Wilderness. 2007. College Station: Texas A&M University Press.

Houston Museum of Natural Science. *Geology Merit Badge Field Trip Guide*. www.abc-cc.com/travel/geology/BoyScout-new-geo-workshop.pdf.

How's the Water? 2011 Basin Summary Report. 2012. Published by Houston-Galveston Area Council in partnership with Texas Commission on Environmental Quality. www.bsr2011.com. [These reports on water quality in the Houston-Galveston area are published annually.]

Huser, Verne. 2000. *Rivers of Texas*. College Station: Texas A&M University Press.

Johnston, Marguerite. 1992. *Houston: The Unknown City, 1836–1948*. College Station: Texas A&M University Press.

Leavell, Lorraine. 1993. *The Original Guide to Family Fishing Holes within 120 Miles of Downtown Houston: More Than 100 Bank Fishing, Jetty Fishing, Pier Fishing and Wade Fishing Locations, Freshwater and Saltwater, No Boat Needed*. Houston: Baylake Publications.

Lower Colorado River Authority. 2003. *A Guide to LCRA Parks and Recreation Areas*. Austin: LCRA. [See also the LCRA Web site, www.lcra.org , which includes paddling trails and maps, streamflow, and lake stage information for the lower Colorado River.]

Moulton, Daniel W., and John S. Jacob. 2000. *Texas Coastal Wetlands Guidebook*. Bryan: Texas Sea Grant College Program.

Nolen, Ben M., and Bob Narramore. 2000. *Rivers and Rapids: Your Guide to Floating and Fishing the Streams of Texas, Arkansas, and Oklahoma*. Garland, TX: Rivers and Rapids.

Norris, Chad W., and Gordon W. Linam. 1999. *Ecologically Significant River and Stream Segments of Region H, Regional Water Planning Area*. Austin: Texas Parks and Wildlife Department.

Parrish, Rob, and Chris Kuhlman. 1993. *Above and Beyond: The Original Aerial-Pictorial Guidebook to the Galveston Bay System*. Bellaire, TX: Above and Beyond Publishing.

Pasadena Hot Spot. 1995. *Boat Fishing Map. Galveston Bay. Trinity Bay. East Bay. West Bay. F102*. Pasadena, TX: Pasadena Hot Spot.

———. 2000. *Wade Fishing Map of West Galveston Bay. F103*. Pasadena, TX: Pasadena Hot Spot.

Ruckstuhl, Eric. 2011. "Paddle Trails Guide: Canoeing Houston's Bayous and Creeks." Bayou Preservation Association. www.bayoupreservation.org.

Surf Cam. www.galveston.com/webcams/.

Texas Commission on Environmental Quality. 2006. *Atlas of Texas Surface Waters*. Publication no. GI-316. www.tceq .state.tx.us/comm_exec/forms_pubs/pubs/gi/gi-316/index. html.

Texas General Land Office. 2003. *Texas Beach and Bay Access Guide*. 2nd ed. Austin: Texas General Land Office. www .glo.state.tx.us/coastal/access/index.html.

Texas Parks and Wildlife Department. 1999. *An Analysis of Texas Waterways: A Report on the Physical Characteristics of Rivers, Streams, and Bayous in Texas*. www.tpwd.state.tx.us/ conserve/sb1/econom/waterways/waterways_indes.htm.

———. 2007a. *Alligators in Texas: Rules, Regulations, and General Information, 2011–2012*. www.tpwd.state.tx.us/ publications/pwdpubs/media/pwd_bk_w7000_1011.pdf.

———. 2007b. *Overview of Laws regarding the Navigation of Texas Streams*. www.tpwd.state.tx.us/publications/ nonpwdpubs/water_issues/rivers/navigation/riddell/.

Texas Parks and Wildlife Magazine. 2006. Special issue: "The State of Wetlands" 64 (7).

Ultra-Graph-Tech, Inc. 1983. *Nautical Charts of the Texas Golden Waterways: Sabine River to the Rio Grande and Connecting Waterways including Ship Channels*. La Marque, TX: Ultra-Graph-Tech.

United States Coast Guard. 2005. "Security Zones for Houston, Galveston, Texas City and Freeport." www.uscg .mil/vtshouston/docs/COTP%20H-G%20Security%20 Zones.pdf.

United States Geological Survey. 2007. "USGS Real-Time Water Data for Texas." http://waterdata.usgs.gov/tx/ nwis/rt.

United States National Oceanic and Atmospheric Administration, National Weather Service. 2007. "Advance Hydrologic Prediction Service." http://water .weather.gov/ahps2/index.php?wfo=phi.

United States National Oceanic and Atmospheric Administration, Tides and Currents. 2011. "Physical Oceanographic Real-Time System. Houston/Galveston Bay." http://tidesandcurrents.noaa.gov/ports/index .shtml?port=hg.

Whorff, John. 2011. *Kayaking the Texas Coast*. College Station: Texas A&M University Press.

Winningham, Geoff. 2003. *Along Forgotten River: Photographs of Buffalo Bayou and the Houston Ship Channel, 1997– 2001, with Accounts of Early Travelers to Texas, 1767–1858*. Austin: Texas State Historical Association.

Index

Other River Books

Paddling the Wild Neches	Richard M. Donovan
The San Marcos	Jim Kimmel
Freshwater Fishes of Texas	Thomas and Bonner
Flash Floods in Texas	Jonathan Burnett
Paddling the Guadalupe	Wayne H. McAlister
Texas Water Atlas	Estaville and Earl
Neches River User Guide	Gina Donovan
Living Waters of Texas	Ken W. Kramer
Exploring the Brazos River	Jim Kimmel
River of Contrasts: The Texas Colorado	Margie Crisp